POT Liquor

Dr. Millicent Thompson

POT

Liquor

Treasure House

An Imprint of
Destiny Image® Publishers, Inc.
P.O. Box 310
Shippensburg, PA 17257-0310

"For where your treasure is,
there will your heart be also." Matthew 6:21

ISBN 1-56043-301-9

For Worldwide Distribution
Printed in the U.S.A.

First Printing: 1998   Second Printing: 1998

The front cover design was taken from "The Tree of Life," an original painting by Keith Mallett of Spring Valley, California. Used by permission.

This book and all other Destiny Image, Revival Press,
and Treasure House books are available
at Christian bookstores and distributors worldwide.

For a U.S. bookstore nearest you, call **1-800-722-6774**.
For more information on foreign distributors, call **717-532-3040**.
Or reach us on the Internet: **http://www.reapernet.com**

Dedication

This book is dedicated to Mom Doris, Grandmom Inez, Grandmom Lonnie, and Great-Grandmom Susie, who are all in Heaven. Thank you for the leftovers. And, to a future mom—my precious daughter Melissa—I leave my leftovers.

Contents

Introduction

This book is about the simple yet profound lessons of life learned in the class-room of everyday experiences. But, more importantly, this book is about the ne-cessity of passing those lessons on to others. I believe that nothing happens to us by coincidence and that every experience is pregnant with a lesson that can teach, enlighten, and bless not only us, but also those who come after us if we learn the value of passing those lessons on.

I am a wise woman who has learned life's lessons well. With grace and in-sight I share some of what I know about love, life, and peace of mind. You may see yourself in these pages. All of our stories have striking similarities. There is a comfort in knowing that others have been where you are. The road of life is not unchartered territory. If you look closely, you will see the footprints of others who have traveled this way and arrived safely at their destinations. Other people whom you have never met have had "just like me" experiences.

Books are written for the purpose of sharing some knowledge, wisdom, ideas, or information with those who may not otherwise walk through the experiences themselves. Like most people, I don't think of myself as having had a life excit-ing enough to fill up the pages of a book—especially a book worth reading. But my keen sensitivity and ability to observe and learn from the experiences of oth-ers give me a wealth of knowledge to digest, assimilate, and pass on.

When I started to peruse my mind, I had no idea that I had so many stories to pass on. I struggled with the writing of this book early on because I could not de-cide whether to use the stories of well-known, "name brand" people or the sto-ries of your "everyday" Jane Doe. I opted to use my own stories and those of everyday people because I found that, regardless of one's station in life, all of our stories are surprisingly the same. I am sure that you have many stories just like mine. Stories are important because they open the heart and rekindle the spirit. Every story is an account of a personal experience that I have had or one that I closely observed in the life of someone else. Stories may be the most powerful teaching tool available to us, especially when the subjects being taught are love, necessary losses, forgiveness, hope, respect, and overcoming obstacles.

Women are nurturers. Collecting our stories is a significant aspect of nurturing. We nurture our families by seriously listening to and seriously considering what they tell us. Listening to, valuing, collecting, and then passing our stories on is perhaps the most important aspect of nurturing. While going through the file cabinet of my mind, I realized that I indeed have more stories and lessons that I have learned from life than could be contained in this one volume. So I have those that stand as milestones to share with you.

Pot Liquor is not for the academician. This is a book for the reader who wants to consider the wealth of wisdom contained in the author's profound observations of life. This is for the person in pain in the pew who could benefit from the wisdom of the Word of God and the time-tested advice of those who have had to tread the murky waters of heartbreak and made it to the shore of healing and resolve. The Word of God is better than a therapist's couch.

This book is a treat for the mind and a treasure chest of insight and inspiration for the soul. Maya Angelou once said, "We must leave some footprints in the sands of life." This book is my footprint. Every impression is evidence that I have traveled this way. As I have walked each road, I have learned many valuable lessons along the way. Those lessons are the valuable leftovers that I pass on to you. Enjoy!

Chapter 1

Setting the Table

Thou preparest a table before me... (Psalm 23:5)

It's Saturday morning and here I am again, standing in line outside in freezing temperatures, trembling while the snow is forming a crown of ice on my raincap. My feet feel like blocks of ice as I think to myself, *Why didn't I wear two pairs of socks? I've been through this before; I know the routine.* It's shopping day in my old neighborhood, and I'm here to buy collard greens. The *neighborhood*, as we have always called it, is intriguing and exciting because of its aromas, colors, sounds, and smells. I look forward to this day every month. It's like a ritual, a sacred pilgrimage.

I know that collard greens are a common vegetable and could be purchased at any supermarket. But there is something special about coming back to the old neighborhood to purchase them. After I take them home and prepare them carefully, following the recipe passed down through my family since slavery times, they seem to taste better than collard greens purchased in suburban markets. I am convinced that it is the memories that are brought to mind when I eat those greens that make them taste better. Every forkful brings to my mind a story that was told or an event that took place as collard greens were being prepared around a pot-bellied stove long before I was born. Sometimes I feel like I can almost hear the conversation that filled those ancient kitchens. The memories are what keep me coming back again and again. My monthly trek into the bowels of inner-city Philadelphia is my opportunity to *reach back* and *reconnect* with my roots.

The buying and cooking of collard greens is almost a religious experience in the African-American community. Back in line, my mouth is watering as the pungent smell of fruits and vegetables call forth sweet memories of days gone by. *Maybe if I hum an old hymn and jump around a little bit, I can take my mind off of how cold I am and how loud my empty stomach is growling.* I'm "ticked off" because the woman in front of me is taking her own sweet time. She's picking over everything and asking a lot of questions. It's obvious that she doesn't belong here. If she did, she would know the routine. She's probably an outsider. *The people who belong here don't ask questions.* We know the difference between a *yam* and a *sweet potato.* Our grandmothers lectured us about the subtle differences between a *collard, kale,* and *cabbage.* If you have to ask questions, it's because you don't belong here. I, on the other hand, am here on a mission. I'm here to buy collard greens and I tell myself, *I'm not leaving till I get what I came for.* With my list in my gloved hand and my money in my pocket, my taste buds begin to "dance in the spirit" as I think about the holiday my stomach will have when those collards greens reach their final resting place in the graveyard of my intestines. There are other items on my list: red onions, salt pork, fresh herbs. But the collard greens are what keep me coming back!

Every time I revisit the ancient Scriptures with its stories and events that are more exciting and intriguing than the most provocative soap opera, I am reminded why the Word of God keeps me coming back. Often times I find myself bubbling over inside at the anticipation of reading the Word or of listening to the incredible exegesis of the Scriptures by a good preacher. That kind of excitement over reading words on a page sounds ludicrous to someone who has not made that journey again and again. But when you've discovered a "good thing," you are compelled to come back for more. Every time I read Scripture, I *reach back* and *reconnect* with men and women whom I have never encountered in the flesh, but who have somehow nonetheless touched my life and memory in a powerful way because I can identify with their struggles. Studying God's Word is like taking a sacred pilgrimage that travels back over thousands of years to look at a situation and learn a lesson from someone else's life without having to leave the comforts of my easy chair.

The Word of God can be likened unto a healthy, hearty spiritual meal that is so nourishing to the soul that it keeps one hungering and thirsting after instruction in righteousness, a hunger and thirst that only God's Word can satisfy. The Lord promises us that this type of "hunger" will always be filled.

Blessed are they which do hunger and thirst after righteousness: for they shall be filled (Matthew 5:6).

Matthew calls those who hunger to read and study God's Word, "blessed." The word literally means *happy, fortunate,* and *blissful.* Here it speaks of more than a surface emotion. Jesus was describing the divinely bestowed well-being that belongs only to the faithful. The Word of God draws me back like a magnet because I have seen its principles and precepts work in my life time and time again. If other believers who approach the study of God's Word with casual interest only knew what they are missing. As believers, we suffer unnecessary distress of every type in our lives because we fail to investigate the nourishing spiritual meal found within arm's reach in the Scriptures. It is like eating at a cheap "greasy spoon," and suffering gastrointestinal distress after every meal because you have not taken the time to investigate the gourmet restaurant just up the street.

The Spice Rack

I live in the suburbs now. I am one of those young, urban professionals who fled the city in pursuit of a better, more comfortable life for me and my family. As a result of hard work and a good education, I was able to "pull myself up by my bootstraps." And as I *got up*, I *got out*. But the city, complete with its crime and counterculture, dirt and danger, draws me back like a magnet. The city of "brotherly love" and "sisterly affection" is an intermingling of cultures and customs. Like the spices on a spice rack, Philadelphia is an unusual mixture of people, culture, and traditions.

On one end of the city, there is Chinatown, complete with a miniature version of the Great Wall. The area is rich in Chinese culture with its pungent smells and gaudy colors. The air smells like a potpourri of oxygen and soy sauce. Men are seen pulling racks of pink, fleshy pigs down the street hanging by the hoof, entrails exposed, and ready for cooking. The back door of Philadelphia's poshest Chinese restaurant swings open as those pigs go in for the first phase of nothing short of a miraculous transformation into a culinary delight. As I think about those pigs, the frown on my face melts into a smile as they bring to mind the many times I have sat in front of an egg roll and a bowl of lo mein fumbling with a pair of chopsticks, trying to fit in. I was trying to look like I knew what I was doing. But the food looks so good, pigs and all, that I forget about trying to fit in and unashamedly reach for a spoon and fork conveniently tucked away in my handbag, proud of myself that I came prepared.

Then there is the south side of the city. They call it "little Italy." The air is so heavy in the shopping areas with the smell of garlic that you would think it was mixed in the cement when the neighborhoods were constructed. Most of the businesses are Italian owned and operated. The people are very friendly but clannish and noisy. Most of them are second and third generation families from Italy and Sicily. They frown upon people of other ethnic groups "invading" their neighborhoods, so there are very few non-Italian homeowners in the neatly, well-maintained row houses that date back nearly a century. Rumor has it that the Mafia is still very active and influential there. Everybody is connected to or knows someone connected to the mob in south Philadelphia. A wise person only goes to south Philadelphia to "look" and "buy" and "leave." Vestiges of a culture found halfway around the globe has found its way into the mainstream of American everyday life. A slice of pizza is more American than Mom's apple pie. Words like *lasagne* and *gnocchi* have crept into our everyday vocabulary. After all, who does not know the difference between a spaghetti, a capellini, and a fettuccine?

Then there is the African-American community. Beneath the layers of smog and urban blight lay the purest survival of the richest culture that has ever graced the planet. The residue of racism and segregation has done great damage here, but in spite of the lack of access and opportunity, the African has demonstrated extraordinary creativity and resilience unparalleled by any other ethnic group in the United States. Brought to this country in shackles and chains, the African was stripped of his culture, traditions, heritage, and names. The brutes who perpetuated the slave trade in America knew the best way to enslave a people is to dehumanize them by stripping away all racial identity and sense of connectedness and community. But the African survived and in many ways thrived in the midst of the oppression and suppression of slavery. Vestiges of rich African culture survived by going underground—but survive it did! The result has been the creation of a perfect blend of two of the world's most divergent cultures, that of Africa and Europe. The end result is a unique melting pot.

Remnants and Vestiges

Every African-American household has certain commonalities that weld us together and keep us united as an ancient people. In every Black household across America, regardless of economic status or educational background, there are common smells and common rhythms that unite African-American people as one. Our ancestors, the Africans, could not bring their language, rituals, and cultural peculiarities to America in their purest form, but remnants of every manner of expression survived in a unique amalgamation of music, art, manner of dress, worship, and food. The hard-driving beat of secular and religious music, replete with syncopated rhythms and rich tonal harmonies, are remnants of Africa. The songs and the singers may be contemporary and updated, but the sound of the drumbeat is reminiscent of ancient Africa. The beat of the sacred and the secular are sometimes disturbingly the same; only the message is different. If it were not for the word *Jesus* every now and then, the creative line that separates the secular from the spiritual in Black music would be even more ambiguous and ill-defined. Music is one of the rich remnants of Africa. Remnants of Africa also show up in every other area of expression in African-American life, but nowhere more distinctly than in the style of preparing, presenting, and enjoying food. No other ethnic group has had such a profound effect upon the cultural fabric of America.

No one will deny that slavery and its tragic residue, racism and prejudice, have done irreparable damage to this country as a whole. Yet an examination of American history shows us that African-American people, when faced with insurmountable odds, found another way. The Africans took their cultural peculiarities to the woods and underground. Vestiges of African culture were preserved in songs and stories around the campfire and in the conversations in the cabins located far enough away from the "big house" where they could not be heard or detected. The aftertaste of pure African culture is savored on the palate of everyday American life. Every major industry has had a taste. Even the fashion industry is not exempt. As an expression of beauty, ancient African women would pierce various areas of their bodies like their earlobes and noses with rings made of precious woods and rare metals. They colored their hair with paste they made from plants, then molded it into elaborate shapes or wrapped their heads in brightly colored cloth. These vestiges of ancient African culture still survive in America today. European fashion models, looking like emaciated rag dolls, float down the runways of some of the most prestigious fashion houses in Europe wearing garments with colors and textures that are reminiscent of Africa. Like the ancient African woman, white girls pierce their ears and noses and eyebrows and any other part of their bodies that will receive such an assault.

What seems new and different and rebelliously modern to dominant American culture is "run of the mill" for African-American women. We have adorned ourselves for centuries. It is an ancient African credo that the human body is God's ultimate masterpiece and therefore should be adorned and put on display for onlookers to visually savor. Who else but a Black woman would sit for eight hours to have her hair braided in plaits so thin that they mimic strands of hair from a distance and then bejewel it with beads and bells and cockle shells? Who else but a Black woman would pay large sums of money to have jewels and beads glued to neon-colored fingernails with a Christmas scene on each nail complete with Santa and all eight reindeer? Some Black women wear earrings that are so big that they decorate their ears like cauliflower or rest on their shoulders like trees. As mentioned before, in African culture the human body is seen as the highest expression of form and beauty in nature. Therefore it is to be adorned, admired, and put on display. European standards of beauty tell us that this is primitive and barbaric. And yet poor imitations are echoed throughout the haute couture lines of every famous or would-be designer in Europe. Vestiges of the beauty and uniqueness of African culture are savored on the palate of every expression of creativity, including fashion, music, and art. But perhaps the most unique vestiges of African culture can be seen in the preparation of food and heard in the telling of stories.

Jello and Stories

I remember as a child going to my friend's house after school, where Mrs. Johnson served us strawberry jello in her set of Tupperware bowls as she told us stories. Mrs. Johnson could talk for hours just as if her only listener was herself. She was absorbed in her stories. My friend and I sat quietly and listened as we swirled the red jello over our tongues. My friend's mother was "weird," the neighborhood people said, because she did not straighten her hair and had lots of wooden knick-knacks of African things all over the house—but she had the best stories. Mrs. Johnson's hair was her "statement to the world," as she called it. She wanted everyone to know how beautiful she thought her hair was in its natural state. I admired her for such honesty. Mrs. Johnson's hair and all of those little wooden knick-knacks were visual reminders of the uniqueness of everything that is African.

My friend thought that I walked her home every day for the jello, but my real reason for walking her home was to enjoy the wonderful stories her mother told us as she scooped out the red, rubbery concoction stuck to the sides of her Tupperware bowls. Mrs. Johnson had the most interesting stories because she traveled and read a lot. She always told us about Africa and how Black people are the smartest and the most beautiful and gifted people on the planet. I loved hearing that. She almost sounded like she was preaching as her voice rose and fell and quivered like the red jello as she talked about Africa and slavery and such, as if she were there. A lot of the things she said I had heard in my grandma's house, just not quite as eloquently.

The older people in my family knew only bits and pieces of information about Africa. But they passed them on just the same in their stories. I learned more about my rich heritage in those afternoons over jello than in all my years in grade school. I learned enough from those stories to know that my Africanness made me unique and special. *I know that the planet is blessed to have me!* Mrs. Johnson and my grandma told me that, and I believed them.

Hand-Me-Down Wisdom

Anyone who has grown up in a family of three children or more knows what "hand-me-downs" are. I grew up in a family of five children. Our life was comfortable enough; we always had a roof over our heads and something to eat. We never complained because we did not know anything different. But like most Black families recently transplanted from the farming communities and the slow pace of the South in the 1950's and 60's, we had very limited resources. There were no summer homes at the seashore and no "spring break" vacations in the islands, no nannies, and no all-day shopping trips. We knew nothing of having privacy and your own separate bedroom. But we never complained because to us there was nothing to complain about. We did not know anything different. My humble beginnings were fine with me, except when it came to clothing. I had no complaints at the ages of seven and eight because I knew no better. But by the time I reached the ages of nine and ten, clothing and how I looked became an area of interest and concern for me.

My mother had a group of girlfriends who all had children around the same age as me. Her friends would exchange their daughters' clothing among each other. To my dismay, I would always end up with a skirt or dress or blouse that had long outlived its fashion trend. My worst nightmare was to appear at school one day wearing one of those "hand-me-down" pieces of clothing and being chided by one of my mother's girlfriends' daughters for wearing a dress or skirt that previously belonged to her. Limited resources made it necessary for my parents to make financial investments in more important things than clothing. "After all," my mother would say, "you'll outgrow everything in six months." And she was right.

My grandmother had an even more extreme opinion. She would say that no reasonable person needs more than two pairs of shoes—one pair for everyday and one pair for church on Sunday. In her thinking, anything else was "frivolous." Grandma's wisdom said, "Clothes are just to keep a person from being naked." So my sisters and brothers and I did not wear signature sneakers and designer dresses and suits. We wore hand-me-downs. My grandmother would turn over in her grave today if she knew how some young people are killing one another over a pair of sneakers or a leather jacket. I appreciate my mother's wisdom because it has helped me to make wise decisions about spending money and avoiding the pitfalls of trying to keep up with others in acquiring material things. Although I no longer wear shoes and dresses until they fall apart at the seams, I do value material things. So instead of throwing things away, I always try to find someone who needs and can appreciate what I have to pass on.

Instead of throwing away the painful situations of my life, I have tried to find people who need and appreciate the lessons I have learned from those experiences. I give those lessons to those who can appreciate what I have to pass on.

This book gives voice to all the old ladies—our mothers, grandmothers, and Aunt Fannies down the street—who passed through our lives and told us their stories and gave us their "hand-me-down" wisdom. Their stories and their wisdom seemed time-worn, antiquated, and outdated at the time of their telling. But upon closer examination, one can see that most of the time those old ladies were right. Grandma and Aunt Fannie told us things that we didn't learn in our schools or read in our history books. But we know those things are true because our grandmommas and grandpapas told us so in their broken English and made-up words, and we trusted what they said. Their hand-me-down wisdom has carried me over some of the roughest terrain in my journey through life. Many times I have encountered seemingly impossible situations, not knowing which way to turn, only to have the wisdom of some "old lady" to come back to me to tell me which way to go. I am so glad that I held on to those stories and the wisdom that came with them. Others may have dismissed those stories as the ramblings of a mind whose thought processes were dulled with age. But those who know like I know hold on to those stories and clutch them to their bosom. We allow them to rest there near to our heart where they are warm and safe until we return to retrieve them so they can give us direction and answers to life's problems.

The "Words" of God

My grandmother's wisdom was always rooted and grounded in the Word of God. Because life is short, we need wisdom that is greater than this world can offer.

We need the "words" of God. If we listen to Him, His wisdom spares us the bitterness of futile human experience and gives us a hope that goes beyond death. Solomon highlights two kinds of wisdom in the Book of Ecclesiastes: a) human knowledge, reasoning, or philosophy, and b) the wisdom that comes from God. Wisdom is the ability to see life from God's perspective and then to know the best course of action to take. Dangers and uncertainties abound in life. Solomon says that a little wisdom will ease the efforts of life. Even though life's experiences often don't turn out the way one would have hoped, wise living usually produces a good outcome. This is a very important conclusion for Solomon's testing of wisdom.

...Wisdom is better than strength.... Wisdom is better than weapons of war... (Ecclesiastes 9:16,18).

Most would agree that wisdom is a valuable asset, but how can we acquire it? In Proverbs, we learn to find wisdom through respecting and honoring God. Wisdom comes from finding God and knowing and trusting Him; it is not merely *the way* to find God. Knowing God will lead to understanding and to sharing this knowledge with others.

So shall the knowledge of wisdom be unto thy soul: when thou hast found it, then there shall be a reward, and thy expectation shall not be cut off (Proverbs 24:14).

The world is full of people who think they know everything. They do not want to be instructed, and they think it shows weakness to learn from others. They are wrong! Listening to others is a sign of wisdom, not weakness. Refusing to learn from others can be a great mistake. It can cause a person who could have been successful to fall on his face.

Apply thine heart unto instruction, and thine ears to the words of knowledge (Proverbs 23:12).

The athlete who thinks—who assesses the situation and plans strategies—has an advantage over a physically stronger but unthinking opponent. And wisdom, not muscle, is certainly what has put mankind in charge of the animal kingdom. We exercise regularly and eat well to build our strength; do we take equal pains to develop wisdom? Since wisdom is mightier than strength, it pays to work on it.

A wise man is strong; yea, a man of knowledge increaseth strength. For by wise council thou shalt make thy war: and in a multitude of counsellors there is safety (Proverbs 24:5-6).

Ancient Mothers

Grandmomma was not able to pass on the uniqueness of her heritage and culture in its purest form. However, oppression fosters creativity—so grandmomma found another way. She and all the other grandmas around her preserved vestiges of their heritage in food, fashion, styles of worship, and the stories they passed on. Those old ladies with their rolled down stockings, their warm, wrinkled hands, and money tucked in their bosom found a way to reach into the future and hold the hand of every daughter who would come after them. They sat around in makeshift kitchens and homemade chairs and they told stories. Their words were syntactically inaccurate and grammatically incorrect, but they were invaluable just the same! So every chance I get, I reach back and reconnect with all the grandmas in my bosom by remembering the things they said as they shared their time-tested wisdom and solutions to life's problems.

There is so much truth in what our grandmas told us, like "Always wear clean underwear just in case you get sick and have to be rushed to the hospital"; "If you can't say somethin' nice, don't say nothin' at all"; "A man who doesn't respect his own mother won't respect you"; "Why buy the cow when you can get the milk for free"; "It's cheaper to keep her"; "A dog who takes a bone will carry a bone"; "Men are like buses, if one leaves, don't panic; another one will come along." These words of wisdom all sound funny and trivial now. But if you stop and think about it, a lot of what those old ladies said still makes sense today. No one can live that long and not learn anything. I have come to understand that anyone who has lived a long time and whose mind is intact enough to tell about their journey is a veritable gold mine of insight and information. There is so much truth in the simple lessons of life.

My grandmother was a jewel in the crown of grandmothers. She, like so many other ancient mothers around her, was a high priestess of the culinary arts. She could take what most people would throw away and create an even better meal that would make one's mouth water. She could make a meal out of pig tails, pig ears, and pig feet. She could take the leftover chicken, chop it up, season it, and call it croquettes. She would take the waste products of a hog like chitterlings, zap it with her ancient magic, and create *wrinkled steaks*. If you are creative enough, you can take what is left over from any meal and make a better meal out of it because there is always something valuable and useful even in leftovers. That is what *pot liquor* is. It is a *leftover*.

Momma and grandmomma worked together. Momma filled a big pot with fresh water. Then she added a pinch of salt to the water. She always knew just how much. All this was in preparation for making collard greens—grandma's specialty. Grandma removed the tie that held them tightly in a bundle, then spread the leaves out carefully. While the salted water was boiling on the stove, grandma washed the leaves of the collard greens and carefully removed specks of dirt and little brown spots left by insects. This process could take an hour— and all the while grandmama talked. The preparation of collard greens is a ritual that should not be conducted in silence. Half the fun is listening to the conversation that it encouraged.

Next Grandmomma added her secret ingredients. Sometimes her secret ingredients were whatever leftovers she grabbed from the cabinet that looked like they would enhance the taste of the greens. But the fat back was the crucial ingredient. Salt pork, the raw, seasoned skin of a hog, is the single element that separates a cooker of collard greens who really knows what she's doing from the ones who are only playing at it. Then Momma added those greens slowly and methodically. They looked like new money wilting in a crystal sea. She cooked them for hours, and the pungent smell filled the house. The smell would creep into the closets and linger there in the wool hats and coats for days. The smell of collard greens cooking in the home had a way of saying, "There is love, and warmth, and safety here," much like the feeling that the smell of fresh coffee gives. No Sunday dinner was complete without collard greens. But as good as the meal was, there was nothing that could compare to the leftovers.

Pot Liquor

When the greens were finished cooking, momma drained the remaining juice off and saved it. The cooking juice from meat is called pan drippings, but the juice from cooked collard greens is called *pot liquor*. To the unknowing eye, pot liquor looks like murky green water fit only to be tossed out. But all ancient mothers know that pot liquor is the richest part of the dish and is worthy of being saved and passed on because it contains the heaviest concentration of vitamins and nutrients needed for healthy growth. Pot liquor was given to the babies and young children who could not chew the greens or who had not yet acquired a taste for this culinary gem. Many times I have watched women in my family put the pot liquor in milk bottles and cups and feed it to their babies. What was thought of as a "leftover" or a "waste product" was actually a valuable part of the meal worthy of being used and passed on.

Whenever I would sit around the kitchen or the living room of those houses in the country listening to sayings and stories my women relatives would share, I thought about the leftovers from those greens. Those stories were the "leftovers" from the experiences of those women. Their stories were vestiges of situations and circumstances that were harsh and life-changing. Thank God those women were willing to save them and share them by telling them to younger women like myself so that we might be forewarned of certain pitfalls in life. Listening to women twice your age tell their stories is a great reminder that nothing ever really changes. The same basic problems in life that our great-grandmothers encountered, those involving relationships, love, loss, disappointment, failure, and indecisiveness, are quite similar to the basic problems we face today. Chances are that what worked for them will work for us with a few minor adjustments. For example, Grandma's advice included:

- Never chase a man.
- Love God first.

- Don't wear out your welcome.
- Nothing good comes easy.
- You can do bad by yourself.

These are all words of advice that have stood the test of time. That is why it is so important to save those stories with the good advice learned from them and pass them on.

The Family Jewels

We often hear people say that when we pass through a difficult life situation and recover from it, we should put it behind us and move on. On the contrary, I think we should tuck those difficult life situations and the lessons we learn from them securely away in our memory like we lock the family jewels in a safe. They are not out in the open for all to see, but we know where to find them when we need then. Memories are like roads: they can take us home again even if only for a moment. We travel certain roads more often than others because those roads lead us to people and places that are important to us—family, loved ones, job, church. Frequently traveled roads lead us to places of purpose. When we go back in our memory with purpose, we can remember valuable lessons that can lead us in better decision-making when we return to the present.

I often go back to the memory of my last conversation with my mother before she went home to be with the Lord. Those words are etched upon my heart forever and chiseled in my brain clearly and indelibly. My mother's words were like a governor's pardon to a prisoner condemned to a life sentence. I will carry them in my heart throughout my life and call upon them whenever I am at an impasse or when I must make an important, life-altering decision. At a particularly difficult time in my life, I was at the crossroads of making a decision to end an emotionally abusive marriage. God had already given me a release, but I would not release myself. I saw and felt the demonic activity in my home. Yet in my mind, I was next in line for the Academy Award for wives. Like many sisters, I grew up living by the Black Woman's Golden Rule: "Do good for others until you collapse." That is how giving and self-sacrificing I was. But because of the wisdom of my mother's words, I learned that even God does not give without expecting, without *requiring*, something *in return*. God blesses us on a daily basis and expects faith and commitment from us in return. When we believe, an exchange takes place. We give Christ our sins, and He gives us His goodness and forgiveness in exchange. What an incredible bargain for us.

For He hath made Him to be sin for us, who knew no sin; that we might be made the righteousness of God in Him (2 Corinthians 5:21).

Like most women before they learn better, I was a people pleaser. I wanted everyone around me to be happy and comfortable and I did whatever I could do to make that happen. So I gave and gave until I had nothing left of myself. That all sounds quite noble, but it wore me down and wore me out to such an extent that I had no time left for Millicent. I remember well the days of exhaustion and the anger I felt trying to please everyone. One day my mother said to me, "Millicent, do what is best for you." Those seven words are the most priceless jewels in my life. They changed the course and direction of my life and caused me to begin to look at every decision I made with new eyes. I still give to others out of the goodness of my heart. But now, when I sense a human parasite in the vicinity, someone who habitually takes advantage of the kindness and generosity of others without making any useful return, I quickly make my exit because I have learned what that can do to me. Now I teach my young daughter how to value herself and how *not* to give away so much of her time that she has nothing left for herself. That is a valuable life lesson! I am forever indebted to my mother for having the wisdom to give me such a priceless bit of advice that was life-changing.

A Cherished Keepsake

Everyone at some time in his or her life receives a gift from someone that is so special that no matter how old one gets or how many other gifts are given, that one remains special. For me, that special gift was a blue taffeta dress. That dress has long since found its way to the trash can, but the precious memory of it will linger with me as if I received it yesterday. That dress had a history, not only for me, but for my mother as well. In its first life the dress was a beautiful evening gown she wore on special occasions when she was "courting" my father, as she called it. (*Courting* is the prehistoric word for dating.) My sisters and I sat for hours while Mother braided our hair and talked to us. She became totally absorbed in her stories. The expressions on her face changed as she moved from subject to subject and event to event in the telling of her stories. Sometimes she pulled out old photographs of her dating days as a teenager. Several times I saw that blue dress in the old pictures. Even in an old, yellowed Polaroid, that dress looked elegant and exquisite. My sisters and I marveled at the notion that our mother was actually a teenager at one time in her life. She did not realize it at the time, but as she told her stories, she also gave us good advice and passed on wisdom about men and relationships that would prove helpful to us in the future. One day while my mother and I were rummaging through one of the many boxes of old clothing we kept in our basement for a steady supply of hand-me-downs, we came across that beautiful, blue dress. Mom was silent as she pulled the dress from the box. She turned her head quickly, but I saw the tears that filled her eyes. When she pulled the dress from the box, it made a loud, swishing sound as she waved it back and forth in the air. When she turned her face again in full view, I watched a wide smile creep across her face as she held it up close against a figure that had long since lost its hourglass shape. Even in her silence I knew Mom was thinking and remembering. As quickly as I could, I struck up a conversation. I wanted to see the dress and touch it and feel it while I remembered my mother's stories. Then Mom made the greatest suggestion she could have ever made to a 13-year-old struggling to leave the kneesocks and braids behind and cross over into womanhood. "Would you like me to make you a dress out of my old dress?" she asked. I was delirious with excitement. I pictured myself looking like a movie star in my first grown-up formal evening dress. I did not have a place to wear it because I was not allowed to date boys, but that did not matter.

For the next several days, my mother nipped and tucked, sewed and stitched and cut until finally the dress was finished. I tried the dress on over a tee shirt and kneesocks. It was a perfect fit. My next dilemma was to find an appropriate time and place to wear it. I could hardly wait to tell my girlfriends about my taffeta dress. I remember using every adjective that came to mind when I described it to them. The day finally came for me to wear my mother's masterpiece. It was a warm Sunday afternoon and I was going to church for a youth activity. I was so glad I did not need an overcoat that day. I did not want my beautiful dress wrinkled or crushed beneath a wool coat. I couldn't wait for everyone to see me. I thought the dress was incredible because it was something precious to my mother and she had passed it along to me. In its original design, as beautiful as it was, the dress was useless because it was not my size. But after a few adjustments it was recycled and became my most cherished keepsake. To my amazement, when I appeared at church that afternoon, my girlfriends were not impressed. In fact, a few of them chuckled—but I did not care. I did not expect my friends to appreciate what my mother had given to me. My mother's stories were a cherished keepsake for me. Her stories are a perfect fit for my life because of the godly wisdom and good advice in them. They are incredible because she took time to share them and pass them along to me.

Can We Talk?

Here I stand in line, rocking back and forth while the snowflakes collect at my feet. The biting cold of the wintry air is almost unbearable. But the wait will be worth it when I get those collard greens. Once again, I quickly take a mental jog through the catalog of my mind, making sure that I have everything I need for the "celebration." No, it's not Thanksgiving, it's not Christmas, and it is no one's birthday. Nevertheless, whenever "the girls" get together, it is a celebration of the highest order. Several of us will get together like our mothers and grand-mothers and great-grandmothers did in times past to "just talk." And talk we will—perhaps far into the evening while enjoying the food I will prepare. Now that's something to celebrate. And no celebration is complete without food. Good food provokes good conversation. Good food is a fitting accompaniment for any celebration or special occasion. So here I stand, freezing and trembling, but

I hold my head high because I belong here. I don't care if somebody from the suburbs drives by and sees me. I am on a mission and *I'm not leavin' till I get what I came for.*

It's my turn! With my list in hand I sidle up to the outdoor counter on feet that now feel like bricks. I quickly make my selections, then abruptly turn, change in hand, bags everywhere, and rush to my van with my treasure. The hard part of this sacred pilgrimage is over. In less than an hour I will be tucked away in the comfort of my own home mixing and measuring, sampling and tasting, while the heavy smell of collard greens and fat back fill every room in my house. Wonderful memories invade my thoughts and a smile creeps on my face as I think about how my own mother and her mother before her engaged in this ritual. I remember, the sight of those collard greens when the cooking was done. Nestled next to the sweet potatoes, they looked like a majestic, green mountain. That sight has a permanent engagement in my memory. As then, nothing today is wasted. We sit around the table and fill ourselves with food and conversation until we run out of things to say. But the greatest joy is knowing that the next day I can open the door to the cold, still solitude of the refrigerator, take out the leftovers of those collard greens, warm them up, invite a friend over, and indulge myself all over again!

As you read this book, digest the information. Absorb it mentally. Allow it to become a part of the storehouse of information you have that will offer you helpful guidance and direction. Good food is nourishing to the body when it is transformed into an assimilable condition. Even so, good information is nourishing to the soul when it is transformed into wisdom that helps us in everyday life.

Enjoy the stories I have selected—from the lean cuisine of love and loss to the meat and potatoes of the tough situations we face in life, situations that challenge our faith and strength. Pull yourself up to the table. I offer you a smorgasbord of situations and circumstances. These stories might seem like "just stories" upon your first reading. But read them over again and again and, after you have reexamined the lessons and the leftovers, they will yield up their secrets.

Chapter 2

The Appetizer

O taste and see that the Lord is good... (Psalm 34:8).

Every good cook knows the importance of serving a food or drink before a meal in order to stimulate the appetite. This appetite stimulator is known as the appetizer. An appetizer can be as simple as a dollop of cheese on a cracker or as fancy and complicated as a spread of caviar or paté on a miniature puff pastry. The fancier appetizers are called canapés or hors d'oeuvres. The canapé sits on its own little couch of crouton or pastry tidbit, while the hors d'oeuvre is independent and ready to meet up with whatever bread or cracker is presented separately. Many hors d'oeuvres are themselves rich in fat. If, before the main meal, the appetizer intake is too extensive, any true enjoyment of the meal itself is destroyed. The palate is too heavily coated, too overstimulated by spices, and too dulled by alcohol. A very hot light soup is a help in clearing the palate for the more delicate and subtle flavors of the meal. The very name *hors d'oeuvre*, literally interpreted, means "outside the main works."

Appetizers should be served in creative and imaginative combinations, remembering that unlike the opera overture, the hors d'oeuvre course should not forecast or overshadow any of the joys that are to follow in its train. Appetizers play an important and functional role, but there is no harm in keeping them simple—just olives, salted nuts, and one or two interesting spreads, so the meal that is to follow can be truly relished. Finally, a good cook will set hors d'oeuvres off with plenty of attractively cut vegetables and garnishes of fresh herbs and greens so that her guests will look forward with great anticipation to the wonderful meal that is to follow.

Spiritual Appetizers

The selection of stories in this book are designed to satisfy your spiritual appetite for wisdom, guidance, and insight from the Word of God as it relates to life. Each story has an "appetizer" at the beginning presented in the form of a wise saying or proverb. Many of these wise sayings are themselves rich in meaning when the reader takes time to savor them. The information in the story itself cannot be fully appreciated by reading the "appetizer" alone. What the "appetizer" will do is stimulate your thinking and encourage you to read on with interest. The authors of these wise sayings and proverbs are obscure. These maxims have been passed down through generations of wise old grandmothers and grandfathers like closely guarded recipes and family secrets so no one receives credit. We just make use of them and pass them on when they are relevant to our present situation.

Every good storyteller knows the importance of sharing a word of wisdom before the story to stimulate the spiritual and emotional appetite of the listener. These "spiritual appetizers" can be as simple as a time-tested word of wisdom from somebody who has "been there" or it can be as significant as the truth and foresight of a profound, all-wise, all-knowing God. Time-tested truths do not change. The intricacies of a story or a situation do not alter the validity of a truth. Real truth is independent and stands alone, ready to meet up with whatever circumstances or situations that life presents.

I am sure that many of you who pick up this book are like me. You are looking for knowledge and information presented in such a creative way that you will take note of it and remember it for posterity. The stories that follow are short and "to the point." I did not waste time or space giving extensive details or minute treatment of particulars. Too much detail would overpower your mental palate. I want to provoke your thinking just enough to provide stimulation for your spiritual appetite.

Some of you are looking for answers to problems you face daily in your homes, families, jobs, churches, communities, and a host of other dilemmas. Some of you are looking for purpose, direction, a cause to champion, or just an opportunity to tear apart an argument. I do not expect you to see every story "my way" or to agree with my perspective. Instead, think of this book as a banquet table filled with a wonderful selection of meats, vegetables, breads, and desserts. Grab a dish and fill your plate. While you select the foods you are accustomed to, be adventurous too and select some foods that are not so familiar. You may discover something new that you like.

There was a time when I could not stomach cabbage. But today cabbage is one of my favorite vegetables because my taste in food has changed and matured and probably because when I eat it now it is prepared and seasoned correctly. The stories and the lessons learned from these stories have been prepared and served correctly because they are seasoned with the Word of God. Pull yourself up to this literary table and make your selections. Perhaps you will see yourself on the plate and decide to make a conscious effort to change thoughts and behaviors that damage your life and hinder your growth. Just as a good appetizer helps you look forward to the main course that follows, I hope you will look forward with great anticipation to the wonderful spiritual meal that follows this appetizer.

Putting Your Business in the Street

Our mothers always warned us about the danger of "telling your business." "Sharing too much information about yourself and your life with people outside of your family could hurt you in the long run because that information might someday be used against you," Mother would say. The funny thing about that was most things we tried to hide and cover up got out anyway. The way I see it, it is probably better to put your own business "in the street" yourself so that the information that travels up the highway is correct. Besides, when we are able to look at a struggle in life as an opportunity to learn and grow, we will no longer feel the need to hide our business as if a life crisis is something that needs to be hidden and covered up. Why cover up information that could prove useful and helpful to someone else?

Some Christians go through life trying to cover up the fact that they are human and capable of making unwise choices and decisions. When I encounter people in church who constantly lash out and condemn others who have certain struggles, I am always suspicious of their motives and curious about their own struggles and situations that they are attempting to cover up. The fact is, we all face struggles. Encountering struggles is a fact of life. Growing and learning from the struggles we encounter, though, is the joy of life. Why some of us feel the need to hold on to that joy is a mystery to me. Joy is enhanced when it is shared with others.

I find the Scriptures to be exciting because everything that is done today has been done before. The Bible is almost like a running soap opera. It contains stories about love, loss, betrayal, worry, fear, doubt, commitment, failure, and other common crises in life. Any connoisseur of daytime television will tell you that the story plot of any modern-day soap opera has a companion in some ancient Bible story. That tells me that there is "nothing new under the sun" (Eccles. 1:9 NIV). Every act of deception and betrayal that brings us so much pain in our lives has been done before. The Bible records it all. God saw the value of inspiring persons to write those stories down so that the lessons learned and wisdom gained from them could be passed on. In God's eyes, people's hearts, their thoughts and motives, are as visible as a lamp mounted in the open. No matter how hard we try to cover up wrong deeds, bad attitudes, and poor choices, we cannot deceive God.

> *For nothing is secret, that shall not be made manifest; neither any thing hid, that shall not be known and come abroad* (Luke 8:17).

Instead of hiding our faults, we should ask God to change our lives so we no longer have to be ashamed. If you are trying to hide anything from God, it won't work. Only when you confess your hidden sins and seek God's forgiveness will you experience God's healing.

Facing Trauma

We all face trauma in our lives, and we stay in traumas until we work our way through them. Carla, a college friend, once told me of the difficult time she had trying to get over the pain of a broken relationship that had ended almost a decade ago. She said that she felt paralyzed and virtually frozen in a time warp. Her solution was to make a calendar starting from the date of her pain. Several times a day she would reaffirm her commitment to herself to get beyond her trauma. In order to do this she would mark a day off the calendar to symbolize getting on with her life. This was a tedious process that took almost a year, but the impact it had upon her life was powerful. Carla was able to put her pain in its proper place—behind her. She was able to bury it and move on. Carla found a way to deal with her problem, but then she had the wisdom and caring for her friends to *pass it on.*

I remember laughing when I first heard my friend, Carla, tell a room full of our friends about her amusing way of putting her problem behind her. It was laughable, but today I think about how grateful I am that she passed that solution along to me. I used it at a time when I encountered a situation that I really had to put behind me. How delighted I am that someone thought enough to pass on what worked for her. That is why there is so much value in sharing our stories with others.

I have always gained a new perspective on a situation when sitting at the feet of my elders. When I was young, I grew to prefer the company of adults over that of other children. I enjoyed my own friends, but sometimes their child's play was boring and predictable. The conversation of the older people, however, was always titillating. I watched the adults interact, particularly the women, because they talked the most. Men could be in each other's company for hours and exchange only a few sentences or nod their heads as they looked off into the distance as they talked. But the women! The women made *eye contact.* And they embellished what they said with colorful words and poignant details that painted pictures in my mind as they talked. I can still remember the very words Momma said that Aunt Agnes said when she found out her husband was cheating on her. I know how Aunt Agnes found out, how she felt, and how she responded because I listened intently to the story while the women talked. What astounds me is that I've heard those same words in the telling of the stories of countless other women since then who went through the same trauma.

Lessons in the Leftovers

Good food stimulates conversation and good conversation stimulates thinking. Good food does more than just delight the palate. It gets one's creative juices flowing and stimulates the brain to want to hear more and share more. There is nothing worse than sitting around a table listening only to the sound of smacking lips and hard swallows while the diners stare blankly at the floor or gaze at the mashed potatoes. Sooner or later someone will *have* to say something. That is why television is such a curse to the camaraderie of family and friends. Television is a killer of conversation. Before I had children, television was a fitting companion and roommate for a single woman living alone. My television never gave me any "back talk" or verbal confrontation. But now I understand the value and importance of healthy verbal interaction with those around me. So I insist on turning the television off when family and friends are around the dinner table so that good conversation is encouraged.

Sometimes the conversation starts off slow—maybe a word here or there during the soup or salad. But by the time the roast beef and gravy make their entrance to the table, the conversation is flowing. What starts out as short bits of information turns into lengthy, colorful stories that can linger well into the dessert. More crucial than the stories, though is the question that sooner or later comes to mind—why did the experience come and what did I learn from it. I have learned more about life over a pork chop than I could have learned relaxing on a therapist's couch. We exchange much of our life experiences and who we are as individuals while poised over food. We act as "griots" who pass along precious information too valuable to be lost and too useful to be discarded as leftover or of little or no worth. *There are lessons in the leftovers.* Just as yesterday's piece of beef can become tomorrow's savory stew in the hands of a good cook who knows what she is doing, so an experience revisited and a story shared can become tomorrow's wise counsel and a tool in the hand of one who is wise and caring enough to pass it on.

The Sacred Place

I am old enough to remember a time before high-tech appliances and gourmet kitchens. Like most modern homes, I have a state-of-the-art microwave that does everything but wash the dishes and sweep the floor when the meal is over. But I still have fleeting memories and faded pictures in my mind of a potbellied stove that stood like a sacred monument in the sanctuary of my grandmother's kitchen.

In times past, the kitchen was always the place where the "high priestess" of the culinary arts would come to offer up the daily sacrifices of food on the altar of a potbellied stove. I remember such a sanctuary in my grandmother's house in the backwoods of North Carolina. It was a sacred place. It was the room in the house that made a house a *home*. Everything significant to home life was centered around what was said and done in the kitchen. In that most sacred of places family wars were settled. Just having conversation over a cup of tea and a piece of dried apple cake helps one to venture back and try to fully understand the source of one's pain. We have all had our blues. Momma would give her time-tested advice while Grandmomma nodded in agreement. Well into the afternoon, a variety of aunts and cousins and other females in training in "the school of life" like me would gather and listen in rapt attention to ancient pearls of wisdom that have stood the test of time.

Granted, most of the time I had no idea what the women were talking about because they spoke in parables and whispered tones and left out people's names. But I knew that what they were saying was important by the look on their faces. So I would find a comfortable spot and sit clutching a doll with no head on it and listen. Years later I would hear those same stories again with the gaps filled in. Curiously, many of those old stories are just like my new stories with the names changed. But the underlying situations are the same: hurt, heartache, betrayal, loss, resolve, and forgiveness. There is something mystical that takes place when one is able to talk things out. Somehow you can separate yourself from the situation for a moment and place it on the table to be looked at and examined and discussed by others. It is very cathartic and therefore aids in the healing process. There is something wonderful in being able to kick back with a friend and say "Giiirrrl!"

Stuff Happens

I laugh now at some experiences that at the time they occurred brought tears to my eyes and much anguish to my heart. My greatest joy is that through it all I was always able to pause in the midst of the emotion to ask the question, "What can I learn from this experience?" Then I was able to answer the question so that the lesson that life sought to teach me was learned indeed. But I did not stop there. I was able to store those life-lessons in the cupboard of my memory so that I could pass them on.

The best lessons are learned through your troubles. A problem is not a road-block; a problem is merely a pause to give one time to ask the right questions. It is a time in one's life specifically designed by God to teach us faith, strength, and patience. Somewhere deep inside we know that we are having a difficult time in order to learn a lesson. There is something we missed "the last time" we were in this or a similar situation. So it comes around again and again until the lesson is learned. Stuff happens and pain is unavoidable. But persistent suffering is something we choose—often simply by choosing to do nothing. If the truth be told, none of our problems—personal or communal—exists without our complicity. We cannot live life without its upheavals. At times we will all feel anxious, frightened, fragile, and out of control. Stuff happens. Our challenge is not to despair, but to keep moving forward despite setbacks and fear and not allow our moods and impulses to control our responses to struggle.

The Usher of God

Pain, problems, and disappointment lead us or push us into a personal experience with God. Life's problems are the "usher of God" that escorts us into a private audience or a one-on-one confrontation with our Creator. Every "way out of no way" situation in life is the forerunner that introduces one to what faith and trust in God really mean. Every "back up against the wall" problem in my life forced me to put into practice every proverb and platitude I had ever heard or learned. Every trial made me reach for what seemed unreachable. My problems and struggles provoked me to ask the right questions, such as these:

"What are You trying to tell me, God?"

"Lord, is this the direction You want me to take?"

"Lord, what am I to learn in this?"

Reluctantly, I admit that my most valuable life lessons, the ones that most prepared me to reach up to God and reach out to people, were those situations that raised the hair on my head, sent a chill up my spine, and caused the acid from my stomach to rise in my throat. But between the chills and the hard swallows I asked the right questions, which gave God the opportunity to give me the answers I needed in order to grow. I remember struggling with the decision to fully commit my life and work to ministry. I had spent more than a decade *after* college educating myself at the finest schools my loan money could buy. I spent many years preparing myself to take a comfortable, tenured seat in the ivory tower of academia. How disturbing to hear the unmistakable voice of God at a time when it was neither wanted nor desired.

That unmistakable voice was calling me to an awesome task that did not fit comfortably into my schedule. God spoke to my heart about starting a church. God did not command or demand my cooperation with this request, however. This let me know that I had the option to obey or to turn my own way and live out my life in disobedience and noncompliance. Unlike many "super saints," I did not "forsake all" and follow. Instead I struggled and wrestled and vacillated for many months. I ran until I had no more places to run. I hid until I had no more places to hide. One morning, while in the midst of one of my most eloquent, well-rehearsed form prayers, God intruded upon my consciousness and confronted me. Then the voices of all those old ladies started crowding my thoughts. Their words came back to me with crystal clarity. I remembered the gleam in their eyes; I remembered hearing the conviction in their voices as those old ladies encouraged me to "stay with the Lord" and "obey God in all that you do." In my thoughts, I talked back like an unruly child. I even argued, but they would not hear of it. It was as if someone turned up the volume of my thoughts without my permission. I knew that a decision to fully commit my life to a calling that was both unconventional, non-traditional, and downright weird would invite trouble. But what choice did I have? Looking back, that confrontation, more than any other, was the "maitre' d" that ushered me into a rich relationship and experience with God that continues to develop and grow as I continue to serve Him.

Chapter 3

The Main Course

This is that bread which came down from heaven: not as your fathers did eat manna, and are dead: he that eateth of this bread shall live for ever (John 6:58).

Eavesdropping is not always a bad thing. I learned a lot of valuable, helpful information as a child while perched behind a door listening to the conversation of grown-ups.

My grandmother taught me how to listen when others thought I was not listening and how to remember what people said when they thought I was not even paying attention. I have avoided many pitfalls and stepped over many stumbling blocks because I listened to other people's stories and heeded the warnings from the life lessons I learned from them. I call them "handed-down stories." I cataloged every gruesome story and filed away every horrible heartache that someone else experienced. I listened carefully to what I heard over the years so that I could recall the stories of others and learn a lesson and so save myself some grief. Handed-down stories from others are wonderful to listen to because one can enjoy the life lesson without the memory of the pain it caused.

As I think about those stories, I tell myself time and time again, *Grandmama was right.* She always said that the past is the past and we cannot live in the past, but we can learn from it. If we keep it fresh in our mind so that we can retrieve the experiences from our memory when needed, then we can look at them with mature eyes and a new understanding and hopefully learn from them and pass the wisdom on.

Old Fools

I do not believe that you should "listen to your elders" just for the sake of listening because wisdom does not come automatically with age. The world is filled with *old fools.* Wisdom comes not with age but with experience—especially when those experiences cause us to draw closer to God. A life without God produces a bitter, lonely, and hopeless old person. A life centered around God is fulfilling. It makes the evil years "when disabilities, sicknesses, and handicaps could become barriers to enjoying life," satisfying because of the hope of eternal life. Being young is exciting. But the excitement of youth can become a barrier to closeness to God because those things that most young people live for—money, popularity, sex, success—take precedence. However, those things become increasingly unimportant with old age.

While growing up I often heard older people talk about how life is so fleeting. For the life of me I could not understand what that meant. My days and weeks were dragging. I longed for the day when I could become an official part of the adult world. I remember dreading Monday morning during my grade school years because Friday and the anticipation of a fun-filled weekend seemed light years away. Now that I am older, time seems to be greatly accelerated. It seems that I am always singing "Auld Lang Syne" and it is the end of another year—again. It is true, time waits for no one. Life is short no matter how long we live. The brevity of life is a theme found throughout the Books of Psalms, Proverbs, and Ecclesiastes. Christ also spoke about it:

> *But God said unto him, Thou fool, this night thy soul shall be required of thee: then whose shall those things be, which thou hast provided?* (Luke 12:20)

Jesus challenges us to think beyond earthbound goals and to use what we have been given for God's Kingdom. Having a clear understanding that each of us has a limited time on earth reminds us that there is still time for change, time to examine the direction of our lives, and time to confess our sins and find forgiveness from God. Because everyone will eventually die, it makes sense to plan ahead to experience God's mercy rather than His justice.

An "old fool" is anyone who spends a lifetime ignoring God and never acknowledging the fact that He alone is our Creator and therefore deserves first place in our life. Many people avoid thinking about death, refuse to face it, and are reluctant to attend funerals. Solomon does not encourage us to think morbidly, but he knows that it is helpful to think clearly about death.

> *It is better to go to the house of mourning than to go to the house of feasting: for that is the end of all men; and the living will lay it to his heart* (Ecclesiastes 7:2).

In my earlier years, like most young people, I never thought about death. I somehow thought I would be the first human born in this century to live past 200 years. No one in my family had died; I did not even attend a funeral until I was well into my teen years. So death was a stranger to me. I remember the first time

I actually touched a dead body. It almost killed *me*. We had just finished a youth meeting at church. (I was about 14 years old at the time.) As we were leaving the church, several gentlemen were bringing flowers into the main sanctuary. They were beautiful and fragrant, so I followed them to investigate. I saw a casket positioned in front of the altar and a man inside neatly dressed in a gray suit. As I trembled with fear, the youth minister of our church, Rev. Long, walked up and suggested that a few of my friends and I go in to see the body. I tried to get away, but Rev. Long grabbed me and dragged me back. Then he gave us a ten-minute Bible lesson about life and death as we stood there frozen and as white as sheets. *This is no time for an impromptu church service,* I thought. Then he did the unthinkable. He told each of us to touch the dead man's face. When it was my turn, I began to cry. I would have given anything to keep from touching that man's face. Realizing that I was not going to get out of this, I struck a bargain with Rev. Long. "I'll touch the man's face if you hold my hand," I said. It was as if I thought the dead man would somehow come back to life and sit up and fuss at me for touching his face. It seems silly now, but my morbid fear of death and dead bodies is common among many people.

Now that I am older, I view death very differently. For me, death is not an *ending*, but the *beginning* of something new, wonderful, and better. I have a very clear understanding of the brevity of this life and the assurance of eternal life. Only a person totally out of touch with reality would think that this life is the end of our existence. I am convinced that my family members and friends who loved the Lord, in this life, are waiting for me in the next life. Because I am so sure of a life after this life, the choices and decisions I make for myself take on new meaning. I do not fear death because I am assured of my next place of habitation. A smile comes across my face as I think about how I jokingly say to my church members, "Just make sure I'm dressed stylishly and look good in my casket, and plan the homegoing service to be a victory celebration."

It is ironic that people spend so much time securing their lives on earth and spend little or no thought on where they will spend eternity. David realized that amassing riches and busily accomplishing worldly tasks would make no difference in eternity.

> *Behold, Thou hast made my days as an handbreath; and mine age is as nothing before Thee: verily every man at his best state is altogether vanity. ... And now, Lord, what wait I for? My hope is in Thee* (Psalm 39:5,7).

Few people understand that their only hope is in the Lord. Blessed is the person who understands these things in his or her younger years.

Chasing the Wind

Solomon summarized all his attempts at finding life's meaning as "chasing after wind" (see Eccles. 1:6). We feel the wind as it passes, but we cannot catch hold of it or keep it. In all our accomplishments, even the big ones, our good feelings are only temporary. Security and self-worth are not found in these accomplishments, but far beyond them in the love of God. Think about what you consider worthwhile in your life—where you place your time, energy, and money. Will you one day look back and decide that these too were a "chasing after wind"? These are hard questions, but ones that I have asked myself many times.

How temporary our lives are! It is as if we are God's guests visiting with Him for a short while before passing on. But while our time here is short, the effects of what we do can be eternal. One well-worn saying states, "Only one life will soon be past; only what is done for Christ will last."

Solomon concluded that even if life is futile, it is still better to be wise than foolish and to live with good judgment than spend one's life in ignorance. Seeking wisdom has definite advantages in this life. The wise man, however, will die like everyone else. Both wealth and wisdom are dead-end pursuits in providing the solution to life. This thought caused Solomon to say that wisdom, while beneficial in this life, is ultimately futile.

Then I saw that wisdom excelleth folly, as far as light excelleth darkness. ... Then said I in my heart, As it happeneth to the fool, so it happeneth even to me; and why was I then more wise? Then I said in my heart, that this also is vanity (Ecclesiastes 2:13,15).

Because we are limited in our understanding, it is important that we come to know God, who is infinite and all-knowing. Solomon realized that wisdom alone cannot guarantee eternal life. Wisdom, riches, and fitness matter very little after death—and everyone must die. We must not build our lives on perishable pursuits, but on the solid foundation of faithfulness to God. Then, even if everything we have is taken away, we still have God, who is all we really need anyway. Death is the ultimate equalizer of all people, no matter what they attained in life. Although this appears to be true from an earthly perspective, God makes it clear that what we do here has a great impact upon where we will spend our eternal life.

For God shall bring every work into judgment, with every secret thing, whether it be good, or whether it be evil (Ecclesiastes 12:14).

For many of us, death is not a reality until we lose a loved one. Seeing a good friend or family member dead in a casket makes you pay attention to your own mortality. When I started out in ministry, I dreaded funerals. For me, conducting a funeral was the most difficult part of ministry. I did not like the sadness and helplessness (and sometimes anger) I saw in people who had lost a loved one. Even when I did not know the deceased personally, I felt sad when I saw and heard others wailing and crying. After many years of pastoring, funerals are still not easy for me, but I find them to be excellent opportunities for witnessing. Some of the people in my church are committed members today because they attended the funeral of a loved one at our church and were met face-to-face with the inevitability of their own death.

No matter what the mysteries and apparent contradictions are of life, you must work toward the single purpose of knowing God. All people will stand before God and be judged for what they did in this life. We will not be able to use life's inconsistencies as an excuse for failing to live properly. To live properly, we need to do the following:

1. Recognize that human effort apart from God is futile.
2. Put God first—*now*.
3. Receive everything good as a gift from God.
4. Realize that God will judge both good and evil.
5. Know that God will judge the quality of every person's life.

How strange that people spend their lives striving for the very enjoyment that God gives freely, as a gift.

Troubling Waters

There are no wasted events in our lives. Every situation and circumstance in the life of a believer happens for a reason and a purpose. Every situation is designed to teach us. When we accept Jesus Christ as Lord and Savior, God puts a plan into action. That plan is a blueprint designed to build Christlike characteristics in us. For each of us the blueprint is different, but the expected end is the same. Our task, then, is to discover what God is trying to build in us when we encounter problems.

Problems are like "troubling waters" that inevitably roll up on the shores of every life. As the water rolls up on the shore, everything in its path is toppled and moved about. The water has a mind of its own. As it rolls back out to the ocean, it takes with it sand and rocks that at first glance seem to be a permanent part of the landscape. Problems roll upon the shoreline of our lives and when the water rolls back out, our shoreline is forever changed. And yet, the tide, just like problems, is necessary and inevitable. The good news is that as a believer in Christ, you are not left to your own resources to cope with problems. God works out all things—not just isolated incidents—for our good.

And we know that all things work together for good to them that love God, to them who are the called according to His purpose (Romans 8:28).

This does not mean that all that happens to us is good. Evil is prevalent in our fallen world, but God is able to turn it around for our good in the long-term. God is not working to make us happy, but to fulfill His purpose. Note that this promise is not for everybody. It can be claimed only by those who love God and who are called. Those who are called are those whom the Holy Spirit convinces and enables to receive Christ. Such people have a new perspective, a new mind-set, on life. They trust in God, not life's treasures; they look to their security in Heaven, not on earth. They learn to accept, not to resent, pain and persecution because God is with them. God's ultimate goal and purpose for us is to make us like Christ (see 1 Jn. 3:2) and to conform us to His image. As we become more and more like Him, we discover our true selves, the persons we were created to be. How can we be conformed to Christ's image?

1. We read and heed His Word.

2. We allow God to teach us through life's struggles.

3. We study Christ's life on earth as our example.

4. We become filled with His Spirit.

5. We do His work in the world.

I Jus' Wanna Testify

"Don't talk so much," Grandma would say. "You can pick up some good teachin' and get some good learnin' jus' by listenin'." Women love to talk. We savor communication and that's good! By nature, women tend to be more verbal than men. Surely every female child comes forth from the womb full of chatter. We are always ready to say, "Fill me in, girl," and, "Then what happened?"

Some people would call that "putting your business in the street." But what good is your "business" if you experience it, learn from it, and then keep it to yourself? I remember being warned about talking too much. Grandmomma would say, "Don't tell all your business. Tell some and save some." In other words, the intricate details of one's personal life is just that—personal. I disagree with that advice because so many others could benefit from just listening to the struggles of others and learning from them. A good friend never keeps anything good to herself (except her man). Your business is meant to be shared with others. That is what testifying is all about. Testifying is sharing the wisdom of a life lesson for the benefit of others. Every one of us, if you have been in church for any length of time, has had the experience of listening to someone tell a story that sounds curiously like one of your own. The very fact that we are still around to share our stories should prompt us to thank God for guiding us through another week, month, and year over the rocky and rough places that you may have doubted you could navigate. I have sat in many church services and listened to well-rehearsed "reports" of how God has blessed someone's life. But those reports were not testimonies because they were not authentic. I laugh when I think about some of those well-memorized, well-rehearsed statements that some people call their "testimony," but that sound more like a worn-out line from an old B-rated movie.

"I thank God that my bed was not my cooling board and my bedclothes were not my winding sheet."

"Thank God for my life, health, and strength."

"He picked me up, turned me around, and placed my feet on a solid ground."

These "sayings" sound good and are familiar to us all who have sat in testimony services for years. But the words are empty and have no impact because they lack substance. We need to be authentic. We need to be truthful in the telling of our testimonies. No one benefits from a sugar-coated version of an experience. We need to tell it like it is. Chances are, our stories are no harsher and no less shocking than the real-life experiences that others are struggling with in secret.

I remember listening to the testimony of a well-liked young woman in our church named Barbara. One evening in Bible study, I sat there wide-eyed, with my ears perked, as she told her story about being involved in an adulterous affair with a married man for almost 20 years. She spoke openly about the pain of betrayal and deception. Barbara talked about the promises this man made to her, how he was going to leave his wife and marry her, and how they were going to live happily ever after. Her story was colorful and juicy as she shared every gruesome detail. She talked about the years of appeasements, like flowers and candy, and of clandestine meetings at her house. I listened intently as she told us how this guy planned vacations where they would meet and how he would spend holidays lying to his family so he could spend a few hours with her on Thanksgiving and Christmas. Then she talked about the pain and disappointment those lies caused and how it took the power of the Lord to break her away from that relationship and give her back her dignity as a woman. It all sounded like a soap opera, but it was real life. To this day, I appreciate Barbara's honesty and openness in telling her story. I needed to hear that this kind of thing happens to real people—to church people. I thank God that Barbara had the courage to share her story—her *testimony*—because it was authentic. Barbara's honesty helped me.

After the Bible study that night, I heard numerous people, male and female, chastise this woman for being "so graphic." One man remarked, "No one should tell everything." One woman said, "She should have kept that part of her business to herself because others will see her in a bad light." *How sad,* I thought *that anyone would even suggest that she be less than honest in telling the "whole truth" about how good God has been to her.* Every time I am approached by some two-timing Don Juan, I reflect back on all the things Barbara said as she shared her story. Most of us don't want to be seen in a "bad light." We don't want others to know that we have made some totally stupid choices in our lives, so we sugar-coat and water down our stories. I thank God that Barbara had the boldness to "tell it like it is" so that I could learn a lesson from an experience she had.

I know it takes a lot of guts to plainly tell what God has done because so many of our stories are shocking. In my own church, when some of the young people testify, they talk about problems that are *real*. Their struggles are serious. They don't talk about failing to make the baseball team or the horror of being sent to the principal's office for chewing gum in class. Today, young people testify about the emotional pain of having an abortion at the age of 15, and of HIV and child abuse and drug and alcohol addiction in junior high school. We cannot afford to tone down or sugar-coat our real testimony or keep it to ourselves until it ends up in the graveyard. We must not add to the wealth of the graveyard. We owe it to the next generation to pass along the treasure of what we have learned from our experiences. Even with all that has bruised us in this life, when the wounds heal, we are still able to feel a sense of triumph when our experiences draw us closer to God. That feeling of triumph can encourage someone else who is walking in the footsteps of your experience. The world needs the life lessons of our experiences for the benefit of our contemporaries and all the generations to follow. The fact that you are reading this book is a testimony that your challenges have strengthened you and prepared you for what's coming next.

GRandma's Quilts

The stories in this book are like my grandmother's quilts—authentic, original, and colorful. My paternal grandmother was born to African and Cherokee parents in the farmlands of North Carolina near the turn of the century. Everything she used was grown in her garden or made by hand. Quilt making was not only a necessity, but also a favorite pastime for women dating back to slavery times.

When winter wind whipped through the cracks of rickety slave cabins, freezing the dirt floors and numbing its occupants, quilting quickly became the means to a very basic end: survival. Scrap material was skillfully used to create colorful patched quilts that protected the slaves from the cold. As the women cut cloth and stitched seams, they sat together and communicated clearly and honestly. When the stories got "juicy" they would look up momentarily, shake their heads, and then return to carefully stitching the quilt. Though years have passed since those first quilts were sewn, the skill has become a tradition and has been passed down from generation to generation and stitched into the fabric of African-American life.

My grandma's stories had color—color like that of a vibrant, homemade quilt. We had quilts everywhere. They were stacked in the attic and in boxes under her bed. They were made from a bunch of rags sewn together in patches. The fabric did not matter, pieces of wool and old lace were neatly sewn in with cotton and satin. There was no attempt to coordinate color or texture. Those old ladies would just use whatever they grabbed first in the rag box. Oh, but if those old rags could talk. If the patches in those quilts could talk, they would somehow share the stored-up words of wisdom that came from those old ladies as they sat around the potbellied stove in that dimly lit, little country kitchen.

That is what the stories are like that we pass down to our daughters. No need to attempt to match and coordinate the information—just tell it like it was in all of its color and texture. There's no need to sugar-coat the details to make the story more palatable to the listener. Something is lost when too much care is given to try to cover up. That is why I am so up-front and forthright in the stories that I share. My grandmother did not care that someone might judge her by judging her homemade work of art. She did not care if you didn't like her quilt or the colors or the direction of the stitching. It was her quilt and she made it to her liking with concern only for the warmth it would provide for the people she loved.

Even so, I am not concerned that someone might judge me by judging the stories I share and the life lessons I pass along. I do not care how you feel about abuse and neglect, betrayal and divorce, and hurt and loss. These are realities that touch and damage people's lives. This book is my quilt that I've made to my liking with concern only for the help that it will provide for someone who might be struggling in these areas. The stories are raw, colorful, and straight-to-the-point. Some stories are frank and brutal—just like real life. I made no attempt to sugar-coat or tone down the horrifying experiences of real people. The beauty of Grandma's quilts was in the unexpected mismatch of every rag that participated in the coverlet. Even so, when one shares a good story, the listener is cheated when the juicy parts are left out. The "juicy parts," like paper glue, are what cause the story to stick in the mind and heart of the listener so that it is there in clear detail when the opportunity arises to retrieve it and "tell it again." When those old ladies sat around in the warmth of the kitchen, their wrinkled hands thimbled and stitching what seemed like 90 miles an hour, it was about more than just sewing rags together. During those conversations, women worked on relationships together. They gave each other advice on how to get a good man or how to get rid of a bad one. Sewing those old rags together gave their hands something to do while they focused their minds and their conversation on working on personal issues and problems.

Grandma's quilts with their "old" smell and faded colors are just a bunch of rags sewn into patches and attached together, but the warmth they still offer make them a priceless treasure when the cold harsh winds of winter begin to blow. Even so, those old stories with their ancient understanding of what is true, right, and lasting still give me guidance, common sense, and good judgment when the chilly winds of adversity begin to blow.

Chapter 4

Soul Food

And Jesus said unto them, I am the bread of life: he that cometh to Me shall never hunger; and he that believeth on Me shall never thirst (John 6:35).

So many aromas emanated from our kitchen that it was rumored in the neighborhood that my family actually invented "soul food." From the days of humble beginnings and the simple lifestyle of my grandmother's house to my present-day existence a million miles from her life, the food remains a constant fixture. I can travel hundreds of miles around the country and visit the homes of African-Americans of all socio-economic levels, and yet the type of food we eat is basically the same.

I remember going to dinner at the home of a very wealthy African-American family. When I arrived, the hired help answered the door and took my coat to hang in the closet nestled among ranch mink and camel hair. I entered the dining room across a long marble floor that was so shiny I tiptoed like a little Chinese lady, hoping I wouldn't fall and hurt myself. I had been invited to dinner along with a dozen other guests. I knew that there would be linen and crystal and other signs of opulence and conspicuous consumption everywhere. And there was. At stations throughout the living room and library there were silver trays of cheeses and fruit and little "fancy, schmancy" pink and green things on crackers. Ladies dressed in uniforms floated around the room with bottles of wine and champagne. I expected to leave the dinner hungry, so I prepared myself. I ate a ham sandwich and a handful of chips before I left home so that my stomach would not growl too loudly at the table. I expected the dinner table to be filled with foods so fancy that they would look more like pieces of artwork, and with dishes of such strange names that I would have to take a risk if I was to try anything.

There I was, positioning myself to take the seat of the beautiful French provincial pink tapestry chair that was offered to me—and it happened. A large bowl of steaming collard greens sat what seemed like a mile down toward the other end of the table. The greens were piled so high in the bowl that they looked like a majestic green mountain rising high and creating clouds in the already fragrant atmosphere. I knew I was "home." Nestled next to the greens was the macaroni and cheese and potato salad. Baskets of corn bread stood in a line like a ceremonial procession leading the way to the barbecue and fried chicken. I should have known. No matter where we go or what we accomplish, certain things, like our food, our music, and our worship, belong uniquely to us.

I pigged out that evening at the dinner party. I left with a smile on my face and a doggy bag in my hand. But the leftovers in the bag were not for the dog. I don't even own a dog. The leftovers were for me. I knew they would taste even better the next day because the taste would be mixed with the sweet memory of a pleasant evening with friends.

No Fads or Fillers

What is "soul food"? Soul food is distinguished from "fast foods" like pizza, burgers, and fries, and from "filler foods" that lack substance like gelatin, celery, and iceberg lettuce. Real soul food has substance—like fried chicken, black-eyed peas, and rice and corn bread. Real soul food makes you sleepy because it is substantial.

I have sat in fancy restaurants countless times eating foods that looked more like artwork than actual nourishment. The carrots were cut like pinwheels. The cucumbers in the salad looked like rosettes, and the slivers of fried potatoes were sliced so thin that they curled up like a satin bow on a Christmas present. Then the plate was decorated with colorful swirls of sauce like an abstract drawing. The meal looks pretty, but it does not satisfy my hunger for food. I have left many restaurants *hungry*—only to go home and have a peanut butter sandwich and bowl of soup to satisfy my appetite.

Soul food is not just a fad or fast food because it has a story behind it. The recipes have been passed down through many generations. Soul food "sticks to the ribs" because it tends to be heavy, and it is heavy because it has substance. Food with substance tends to be more nourishing for growth and life.

The stories in this book are not meant to be space fillers. They are harsh and shocking. Some are repugnant and ugly just like real situations in life. Just as soul food sticks to your ribs, I want these stories to stay in your mind. I don't want you to read this book only to be left spiritually hungry. I want you to come away from the table with a clear understanding of the relevance of Scripture to every situation that confronts you in daily life. Wisdom from God's Word is "heavy" because it has substance. The substance of God's Word is the wise counsel, good advice, and guidance that it offers. Good advice and wise counsel is spiritually nourishing for growth and life. Listen to advice and accept instruction, that you may gain wisdom for the future.

Hear counsel, and receive instruction, that thou mayest be wise in thy latter end (Proverbs 19:20).

In this age of information, knowledge is plentiful, but wisdom is scarce. Wisdom means more than simply knowing a lot. It is a basic attitude that affects every aspect of life. The first step to wisdom is to fear the Lord, to honor and respect Him and to live in awe of His power. The Bible is our standard for testing everything else that claims to be true. It is our safeguard against false teaching and our source of guidance for how we live. Paul told Timothy that all scripture is inspired by God and is useful for teaching, for rebuke, for correction, and for training in righteousness, so that everyone who belongs to God may be proficient, and equipped for every good work.

All scripture is given by inspiration of God, and is profitable for doctrine, for reproof, for correction, for instruction in rightousness: That the man [woman] of God may be perfect, thoroughly furnished unto all good works (2 Timothy 3:16-17).

God wants to show you what is true and equip you to live for Him. The Bible is not a collection of stories, fables, myths, or merely human ideas about God. It is not just a human book. Through the Holy Spirit, God revealed His person and plan to certain believers, who wrote down God's message for His people. This process is known as inspiration.

Knowing this first, that no prophecy of the Scripture is of any private interpretation. For the prophecy came not in old time by the will of man: but holy men of God spake as they were moved by the Holy Ghost (2 Peter 1:20-21).

The Bible is God's very words that were given "through" people "to" people. The writers wrote from their own personal, historical, and cultural contexts. But even though they used their own minds, talents, language, and style, they wrote what God wanted them to write. Scripture is completely trustworthy because God was in control of its writing, and its words are entirely authoritative for our faith and lives. Read it and use it to guide your conduct. God wants to show you what is true and equip you to live for Him.

Read these stories with a heart and mind that are open to what God wants to say to you. Pray this prayer:

Lord, give me understanding and spiritual insight into the truths of Your Word. Help me to know that Your Word is true and relevant to my life and to the situations that confront me. Help me to apply Your Word to my life so that I may grow. I want to discover Your truth and become confident in my life and faith. Even if the truth hurts, I am willing to listen so that I can more fully obey You. Amen.

Stoop Ladies

When I was growing up, every Sunday was like a holiday. Everyone would gather at "the house" after church to eat and talk as families do. "The house" was any designated location where the adults gathered with their children to eat Sunday dinner. It could change from week to week. Sometimes the Sunday family dinner was held at church during special days like Easter and Christmas. Regardless of the changing location, one thing remained stable: the food. Basically, we always had the same food items. But no one ever complained. Everyone always agreed that in order to have an authentic Sunday dinner there must be chicken or collard greens somewhere. Wonderful smells filled the house. My mother, grandmother, and a variety of cousins and aunts celebrated life's milestones in the kitchen. When I was a little girl, I loved watching and listening while I sat under the kitchen table. The best of my collection of stories were heard under various kitchen tables at those Sunday dinners.

When Sunday dinner was over and the dishes were done, the women would take the conversation outside to the front porch. I would try to find an excuse to go outside with them, so I would ask my great-grandmother to braid my hair. I would sit there nestled between her knees, leaning against legs that had walked the narrow corridors of many tabacco fields in North Carolina. I loved "braiding" times. They were special times that we spent with our M'dear. "M'dear" is a nickname for mother or grandmother in the Black community. The name embodies all the love and warmth a word can hold. Any wise woman who "took you under her wing" and mentored you as a young woman became your "M'dear." There were many M'dears in the community. But mine was special because she belonged to me. Braiding times were times of listening and talking. I loved those times because whoever braided my hair that day was a captive audience. I could talk about anything without fear of distraction. No subject was taboo, and I appreciated that.

Many years later when I moved to the inner city of Philadelphia, I was grateful to see that the art of conversation among women was not lost. Instead of sitting on the front porch, the women gathered on the steps. They would sit on the stoop where they could reprimand and monitor everyone's children, spank a few if they had to, and just talk. As the warm, humid air of a Philadelphia summer became the crisp, cool air of autumn and the vibrant, green foliage turned yellow and orange, the "stoop ladies" would sit there talking. It seemed as though they never left, as if their stories were one, long, continuous story. When the harsh winds of a Pennsylvania winter chased them indoors, they would gather again in their kitchens or on the telephone to talk.

When I became a teenager, the women would let me participate in those con-versations. I appreciated that. While I talked, I was also listening and learning. I was learning lessons that I knew would help me later in life. Sometimes one of the older women would share a heartbreaking story with everyone on the stoop. Her cheeks would become wet with tears as she talked about some struggle in her life. In the midst of the conversation there would be a "thinking" silence. Then someone would always interject something about God or the Scriptures to bring clarity to a difficult situation. Someone in the group would always share some "wisdom" from the Word of God that let me know that scripture is relevant to every circumstance we encounter in life.

There are basic biblical principles and scriptural truths that do not change. The details of difficult circumstances change, but the wisdom to handle them properly never changes. Truth is timeless, and all truth is rooted in the Word of God. Truths about life are unchangeable, like oil in water, whose drops remain unchanged despite the volume of liquid around it. The oil of God is unique in that way. The stories and the leftovers in this book are presented to you to show you how the Word of God is relevant to everyday human crises and situations. As a result, you will see how crucial it is to saturate yourself with the Word of God if you are to have a successful life. Saturating yourself with the Word of God is like pampering your palate at holiday season with second helpings.

The Joy of Sharing

The women in my life who have become my best friends are those with whom I share my secrets. Good conversation has a way of bonding people to-gether. I have so many wonderful memories of sitting in my living room or dorm room with friends sharing conversation. Good conversation informs, challenges, confronts, and renews. We held hands or leaned on each others' shoulders, crying, as we listened to each others' stories of heartbreak and peril. But I also have memories of laughing after the tears dried up. Sitting around as friends, we did not just listen to the stories; we also felt compelled to put our two cents' worth in. We would end up giving counsel to one another. We were not always right about the solution to problems, but *the joy was in the sharing*, just as a meal tastes bet-ter somehow when shared with friends.

Good food that is well-seasoned and prepared with love and care restores, re-vives, and builds up the physical body. Likewise, good *spiritual* food informs, challenges, confronts, and renews. The meat of the Word of God puts substance to the bare bones of life's struggles. The skeletons that rattle in our closets can now be taken out and quieted down because we no longer have to keep them quiet and hidden. We can talk about the "stuff" that some people think we should keep hidden and not talk about. We can "put our business in the street" because the fear of exposure is no longer there. I can share my stories and the stories of others because, as painful as they were at one time, I have come to a place of healing and resolve. One comes to a place of healing and resolve because there is closure. The lessons that God wanted me to learn and the characteristics that God wanted to build in me were accomplished.

Selections from the Menu

I could very well be accused of choosing extreme stories for this book, but life is extreme—a mixture of the absurd and the sublime. Life can be distasteful at times because it is painful, yet it is also original and thrilling. I have chosen those stories that will delight and challenge your spiritual appetite. Maybe you have a taste for something light just to take the edge off your feeling of hunger or maybe you desire something heavy that will stick to your spiritual ribs. Whatever your palate desires, these stories are sure to mirror experiences you have had or will have in the furure. Stories stimulate one's appetite for thought, examination, and thinking. I want you to want to turn the page. I want these stories to elicit some kind of emotional response. Go ahead and break down. A breakdown can lead to a break through. Let the words marinate. Maybe by the end of this book you will feel like sharing some of your own stories with someone else. Turn up the volume of your life and tell your own stories.

I have discovered that many people who seem to be moving through life without a care in the world are suffering from a lot more hurt than most of us realize. The smiles on their faces are covering a flood of tears in their hearts. They were abused as children. They have been hurt by a stranger, a relative, a spouse, or a friend. They have experienced the rejection of a divorce; their character has been maligned; they've been given a raw deal at work; they've been betrayed by a spouse.

Some of the hurts that we receive are only minor in nature. They amount to nothing more than day-to-day bruises and need to be brushed aside as quickly as they arise. They have not been intentionally inflicted, nor are they all that serious in nature—like a careless word or an embarrassing remark made by a friend. Some hurts are going to come our way in the normal course of day-to-day living. It's the price we pay for being alive. These kinds of hurts should require nothing more than a Band-Aid and a little time to heal. There is no point in making a mountain out of a molehill or a federal case out of a misdemeanor. We should be mature enough to cast them aside as quickly as they arise.

I wish I could say that all the hurts we receive are minor hurts, but they are not. Many of them are far more serious. They cause great pain and require a lot more than a bandage to heal. Some of the hurts that we receive are more like open wounds than insignificant bruises. The pain that they cause is deep and lasting. Unfortunately, we cannot *pick and choose* the problems that we encounter in life like we make selections from a menu. Stuff happens! If we fail to cope with these hurts adequately, with the intention of learning and growing from them, they will breed anger, resentment, bitterness, malice, suspicion, distrust, hatred, cynicism, and fear in our lives like the mold that spreads rapidly on a piece of stale bread and destroys its taste and viability. How effectively we cope with these kinds of hurts will determine our level of growth in the Lord and our emotional health.

In order to enjoy a good meal, utensils are usually helpful. Utensils, such as spoons, forks, and knives, are tools that we use to cut our food up into bite-sized pieces so that it can be chewed, savored, swallowed, and used as nourishment for our body. Utensils are not necessary. Any meal can be eaten with our hands, but a spoon, fork, or knife makes it easier and more comfortable to digest the food. Every story and lesson in the spiritual meal that follows also has a "utensil" in the form of a verse of Scripture or a wise saying. You can use these as tools to prepare your mind to fully digest the spiritual food that follows. Then there is a "tidbit of wisdom" at the end to encourage you to think even more. Enjoy!

Story 1—Finding Fuel in Failure

The Story

*A well-trained memory is one that permits you to
forget everything that isn't worth remembering.*

Denise was haunted every day of her life by the decision she made as a teen-ager to take a drag on that first cigarette of marijuana as she stood against the wall at a party. She knew the risks. She had been properly lectured at home and at school about the perils of experimenting with illegal drugs. But she was different from everybody else. "I won't get hooked," she would brag to her friends. "I'm too smart for that." Now Denise sat in my office some 20 years and many other bad choices later, head in hands, crying about the wasted years, the wasted opportunities, the broken marriage, the months of rehab, and the alienation from her family and friends. "You cannot go back, but you can go on," I told her. Denise worried about what others would say when they learned about her past. She had finally gotten to a level of spiritual maturity where she wanted to ac-tively participate in the ministry of our church in a leadership capacity, but she worried about the whispers and finger-pointing that she knew she might have to encounter. The pain of a past that she feared might catch up with her was so great that she had come to me as her pastor to say that perhaps it was best she remain in the background as a spectator and not become a participator in the church.

The Life Lesson

...Neither do I condemn thee: go, and sin no more (John 8:11).

If a choice turns out to be something that you later regret, you must let it go. Try not to blame yourself because you cannot call things back. If you do, it comes with a price. Wasting precious moments in life regretting our bad choices is like spending time trying to capture the echo of a bad word after it has been spoken. We have all made choices in our lives that have left a horrible aftertaste on the palate of our future. I remember the first time I tasted caviar. I was in an elegant restaurant with linen tablecloths, crystal, silver, and a handsome gentleman. I had heard so much about how tasty, rare, and expensive caviar is that I could not wait to get my first taste. One spoonful left me gagging, nauseous, and groping for a napkin. I know that caviar is fish eggs, but I did not expect such a vile, repugnant taste. I quickly excused myself to the ladies room, rinsed my mouth out, brushed my teeth, pulled out a peppermint from my handbag, and got rid of all vestiges of my first *and last* experience with such a delicacy. Then I moved forward to enjoy the rest of the meal with no thought or lingering aftertaste of caviar.

John writes in chapter 8 that one morning Jesus was in the temple teaching the people when the scribes and Pharisees brought in a woman caught in adultry. They demanded that she be stoned for her crime according to the Law of Moses. In an effort to challenge Jesus and accuse Him of transgressing the Law, they questioned Him as to what should be done with the woman. Instead of answering, Jesus stooped down and wrote something on the ground with His finger, as though He did not hear them. So when they continued asking Him, He raised Himself up and said to them, "He that is without sin among you, let him first cast a stone at her" (Jn. 8:7b). Then again Jesus stooped down and wrote on the ground. At that point, those who heard Jesus' words, being convicted by their conscience, left one by one, beginning with the oldest. Finally Jesus was left alone with the woman standing there. He said to her, "Woman, where are thine accusers? hath no man condemned thee?" (Jn. 8:10b) When she replied that no one had accused her, Jesus told her, "Neither do I comdemn thee: go, and sin no more" (Jn. 10:11b).

The woman whom the Pharisees and scribes presented to Jesus must have been utterly humiliated at being dragged into the temple by self-righteous men who were only using her to try to trick the Teacher they hated. Jesus refrained from challenging their hypocrisy, but He did set a new standard for judgment: Let someone perfect decide the case.

So when they continued asking Him, He lifted up Himself, and said unto them, He that is without sin among you, let him first cast a stone at her (John 8:7).

Ironically, Jesus was the only one who fit that qualification, and He did decide the case—declining to condemn the woman, admonishing her to "go, and sin no more."

A Tidbit of Wisdom

Perhaps, like this woman, you have experienced the forgiveness of God for grave offenses against His holiness. If so, live in His grace—and sin no more.

Story 2—Overcoming Worry

The Story

Worry is a gravedigger that has no mercy.

Christine was the "queen of worry." She earned the title honestly. She would worry about things that would probably never happen. Most of the things she worried about were created in her own mind. She even worried about worrying too much. One day as a group of friends were sitting around some hamburgers and fries, what started out as a pleasant conversation turned ugly when Christine began to chime in.

She announced to everyone that she was scheduled to enter the hospital in a week for a series of tests in order to properly diagnose a series of symptoms that she was having. She complained of sleepless nights, upset stomach, lack of appetite, thinning hair, and a general feeling of hopelessness. "Everything is going badly," she said, "and I'm worried sick." "Could it just be," one friend responded, "that because you are, as you say, 'worried sick,' you are applying sick and irrational thoughts to your affairs and therefore making them go badly?" But Christine persisted. "Everything is washed up, finished," she moaned. "My life is as good as over, with nothing but a mess of worries."

"I'm sorry to hear that your husband has left you," one friend said sympathetically. "Who said he has left me? My husband loves me and sticks by me," Christine retorted. Then the friend added, "It's too bad your children are no-account drug addicts and in jail. And I'm sorry to hear that your house burned down and your insurance lapsed." Christine interrupted, almost insulted, saying, "My children are not dope addicts! They are good kids who have never seen the inside of a jail. And my house did not burn down, nor has the insurance lapsed. In fact, all our bills are paid, and we are planning on taking a much-needed family vacation to the islands this winter, but I'm worried about the weather. A lot of hurricanes and tornadoes have caused destruction in the islands in the last few years." By this time, however, Christine had gotten the message. She realized that she was so focused on the "bad" that might be, that she could not focus on the "good" that was.

The Life Lesson

Cast thy burden upon the Lord, and He shall sustain thee: He shall never suffer the righteous to be moved (Psalm 55:22).

Your physical mechanism is sensitive to whatever goes on in your mind. Since worry is located in your mind, it can have a devastating effect on all the parts of your body. My grandmother called it "worriation." We are all familiar with the physical feelings. It is a pounding in your head or a knot in your stomach that won't unravel. It's sweaty hands in cold weather and chattering teeth in balmy temperatures. Oh yes, the physical body reacts.

A worried thought cuts a thin trickle or rivulet across your consciousness. Repeated, it deepens into a channel of fear or anxiety. Every thought comes up tinctured with worry. As a result, you become a person of fear, a confirmed worrier. You have, by this process, created a *mental climate* in which worry thrives and grows and finally takes over, dominating your entire life experience. To arrest this tragic process, you must reconstruct your worry-conditioned mental climate by gradually substituting a spiritual climate. This can be done by inserting into your consciousness a fresh new system of thinking. A physician's prescription uses the symbol Rx, which means, "Take thou." So I would suggest that you "take thou" the Word of God into your mind. Give your troubles to God; He will be up all night anyway:

Let the Word of God dissolve deeply into your conscious control center where your life pattern is formed. It will, if tenaciously held there, drive from your thoughts the infections that have for so long fed the disease of worry. Here are four ways to check your worry habits:

1. Start being absolutely honest with yourself. When you hear yourself making a negative statement, ask yourself, "Do I honestly believe what I am saying, or am I mouthing negativism that I do not really believe at all?"

2. Carefully practice listening to yourself. Note and study with meticulous attention every comment you make, so that you might become fully conscious of the amazing number of doleful and negative remarks you utter.

3. Keep track of everything that happens as you work this new procedure. Carefully note and compute even the smallest results. Tell yourself, "Things are going great!" even when they don't seem to be.

4. Practice putting the best connotation on the words and actions of every person and every situation. Such a practice actually helps stimulate a good outcome. Always seek to think the best results in enthusiasm for people, for business, for church; it helps one toward a worry-free life.

A Tidbit of Wisdom

Add up your blessings to subtract your worries. Blessed is the man who is too busy to worry in the daytime and too sleepy to worry at night.

Story 3—Surviving Loss

The Story

Death is always a wake-up call to remind us that life
is fragile and death is totally out of our control.

Linda's Story

My mind was racing as I sat there feeling like a character playing a part in a melodrama that was not real. I was physically and emotionally exhausted. A long line of friends and relatives had visited. Still more waited in line to express their condolences at my husband's death. I am perplexed because bad things are not supposed to happen to good people.

Gary and I were married for only two and a half years when what began as a back pain became the most virulent form of cancer. As we sat in the emergency room, I kept telling myself, "Gary can't be that sick." I was only 26 years old, a new bride, and looking forward to the fairy tale of life that every girl dreams about: the great husband, children, and the house with a white picket fence. Gary's lymphoma seemed like a betrayal from God, and I was mad. After all, I did nothing to deserve such a rotten break in life. All our dreams were taken away. Neither of us prayed to God. We were so numb that we just wallowed in the shock of it all. I felt like I was on an emotional roller coaster. Sometimes I would scream obscenities into a pillow. Gary couldn't help me through my grief; he was overwhelmed with his own. His own anger was incredibly strong, as if I had done this horrible thing to him. I tried to give him his space, but sometimes we were like two angry missiles determined to destroy each other or to at least "get even" with words.

I feel like I spent a year of my life trapped in a nightmare. Alcohol gave me a respite from my confinement. It was a great escape. Sometimes when I prayed, I begged God to take Gary because the pain of watching him slip away was just too much. I moved into the hospital to be closer to my husband. I became so accustomed to the chemotherapy, the doctors, and the slow walks up and down the oncology floor in the late night hours that people in the hospital thought I worked there. Members of my family urged me to go home. They thought I was not taking proper care of myself by living around so much sickness and death. They didn't realize that I was taking care of myself by being close to someone whom I loved deeply.

After a successful bone marrow transplant, ten months after his diagnosis, Gary went into remission. After so much talk about death, this seemed almost too good to be true. Cancer was our "Gary and Linda experience." We didn't easily open up to others, so we told no one about this new development. We had so completely prepared ourselves emotionally for Gary's death that the news of his remission seemed almost anti-climatic. I had purchased a cemetery plot earlier that summer and prepared my heart for the inevitable loneliness of widowhood—and now remission! However, Gary's remission lasted only a few weeks before the symptoms began to reappear. Excruciating back pain signaled that the lymphoma had come back. We held each other and cried, and I cried alone a lot. There were times when Gary and I tried to get on with our lives. We refused to allow this monster to invade our lives and destroy our dreams. But somehow, even before we were married, I sensed that my time with Gary was limited. I don't know how or why I knew; I just knew.

Now when I look back, I know that God planned Gary's short time of remission because we still had unfinished business. I needed that time to reflect. My husband's illness, as horrible as it was, taught me something about love. I knew that my husband loved me and I loved him, but I never really knew until then how deeply and unconditionally he loved me. I learned something about the depth and breadth of God's love that I would have otherwise not known.

I knew that Gary wanted to die at home. After being home for several weeks after Christmas, Gary finally slipped away peacefully in our bedroom. People often tell me how lucky Gary was to have me, but I was so tremendously blessed to have had him. Gary showed me how much God loves me. Our meeting was divinely ordained. For the first time after this experience I was able to say, "God, I love You," and understand what that means.

The Life Lesson

Yea, though I walk through the valley of the shadow of death…Thou art with me… (Psalm 23:4).

Loss is a challenge, and as with any challenge, it opens the way for growth and change. Many times we do not realize how precious we are to each other until one family member becomes a memory. Family members are gifts to each other. When my own mother became ill, my need to be with her, to comfort her, and add some joy to her otherwise pain-filled days, compelled me to make room in my pressured, overcrowded days. Nothing short of the pain and grief I felt watching her slip away could have taught me to control my schedule and not allow it to control me.

Death casts the most frightening shadow of all over our lives because we are the most helpless in its presence. We can struggle with many other enemies—pain, suffering, disease, injury—but we cannot wrestle with death. It has the final word. Only one person can walk us safely through death's dark valley and bring us through to the other side: the God of life, our Shepherd. With the time of our death uncertain, we should follow this Shepherd with an eternal confidence.

Yea, though I walk through the valley of the shadow of death, I will fear no evil: for Thou art with me; Thy rod and Thy staff they comfort me (Psalm 23:4).

When someone close to us dies, we need a long period of time to work through our grief. When Jacob died at the age of 147, Joseph wept and mourned for months.

And when Jacob had made an end of commanding his sons, he... yielded up the ghost, and was gathered unto his people. And Joseph fell upon his father's face, and wept upon him, and kissed him (Genesis 49:33–50:1).

Crying and sharing our feelings with others helps us to recover and go on in life. Allow yourself and others the freedom to grieve over the loss of a loved one, and allow a long enough time to bring grieving to completion.

Figuring out what to say or how to be of help to a friend who is grieving is not easy. But to do or say nothing is to deny the loss. This can cause a mourner pain and confusion, as he or she may wonder whether you are even aware of the death. What, then, can you do to show your concern and to help ease someone else's burden? Here are some ideas.

- Share a memory of the deceased person.
- Listen much; say little.
- Deeds of kindness speak for themselves.

Those "I remember when" stories can be precious to a family. If you did not know the deceased person well enough to have a memory to share, you can, when the time is right, invite a grieving person to share a story with you. This lets the grieving person know that you do not intend to forget the one who is gone, and it can bring comfort to your friend to be able to talk about some of the things that made the loved one special.

Sometimes all you can say is, "I'm sorry. This must be so difficult." Beware of saying, "I know how you feel." The most compassionate thing you can do is convey the idea that you know the person is hurting, that you care, and that you want to help if you can. People who are in the early stages of grief often don't need to hear a lot of words. Rather, they need to sense your presence and your support. They are more likely to need to talk than to listen, so don't worry if you feel at a loss for words.

Acts of kindness speak for themselves. One of the nicest things that can happen to a grieving family is the appearance of good friends at the front door holding a tasty meal. Providing food at the time of a death is supportive, but doing so later is also good. About two weeks after the funeral, all the cakes and casseroles are gone. Also, offer to run errands or do some necessary shopping in those first hectic days. Buying milk, putting the trash out, or filling the car with gas are things that the family may not feel like doing. Consider doing something like this in place of purchasing flowers or some other memorial. Remember, flowers wilt, but human needs continue.

If death ended it all, then enjoying the moment would be all that matters. But Christians know that there is life *beyond* the grave, and that our life on earth is only a preparation for that life. Death is not the final word. For those who believe in Christ, death is only a prelude to eternal life with God. Our lives will continue, both in body and in spirit. Let this confident hope inspire you to faithful service.

We are confident, I say, and willing rather to be absent from the body, and to be present with the Lord (2 Corinthians 5:8).

It helps to consider that our loved ones are happy—free of pain and hassles—and that we will be together again.

Thou has turned for me my mourning into dancing: Thou hast put off my sackcloth, and girded me with gladness (Psalm 30:11).

Also, if you died, would you want your loved ones to deeply mourn the rest of their lives? No, you want them to enjoy life as much as possible. Your missing loved one wants this for you now. During those most difficult times when your sense of loss seems unbearable, pray this prayer:

Lord, help me to know that You see my tears and feel my pain. Give me the peace that passes all understanding. Help me to know that michael is happy with You. Thank You for the good things that he/she brought to my life. In time, restore laughter in my life and joy in my heart. Amen.

A Tidbit of Wisdom

Healing does not mean forgetting, and moving on with life does not mean that we don't take a part of our loved one with us.

Story 4—Diffusing Hatred

The Story

Hating people is like burning down your own house to get rid of a rat.

Rev. Jackson's Story

Eleanor had a "gift" for saying the wrong thing at the wrong time in front of the wrong people. Eleanor was a very insecure young woman, so she always maintained a safe distance from other people. On the surface, she seemed outgoing, almost gregarious. But deep within, she carried the wounds of years of being told she was ugly and dumb. Many years of negativity and criticism resulted in a damaged ego, poor self-image, and low self-esteem.

Eleanor learned to cope with her problems by being very critical of other people. It has often been said that a child who grows up with a lot of criticism learns to criticize. It has been at least ten years since Karen, Eleanor's one-time best friend, became the sacrificial lamb of one of Eleanor's cutting remarks, and it happened in church. We were in the company of a room filled with friends. This was the fellowship hour just before church service, and as many people do, we congregated with other people in our age group to greet one another and talk about the events of the week. Karen was wearing a beautiful red suit with a brightly colored silk scarf. She had seen the suit in a department store window two months earlier and fell in love with it. It was cut just right, the fabric was exquisite, and the color was lively and vibrant—just like Karen. After four months of waiting for it to go on sale, she finally brought it home. *This Christian life does have its "perks,"* she thought.

Everyone was laughing and talking and enjoying one another's company. Just then Eleanor walked into the room. After greeting a few people she caught a glimpse of Karen across the room and proceeded to walk over briskly as if she was drawn like a magnet. After exchanging a few pleasantries, Eleanor looked at Karen up and down as if she was inspecting every seam and thread of her outfit. I thought nothing of it as I watched. I admired the suit too. Women enjoy admiring other women's clothing.

Then Eleanor said, within earshot of everyone, "Your suit is very nice, but the color is provocative. A real Christian woman would never wear something so enticing because her mind is on God and not on trying to attract the attention of others." There was a graveyard silence in the room. Granted, Eleanor's remark was foolish and uncalled for, but that did not lessen the hurt and embarrassment Karen felt.

Karen bolted from the room as quickly as Eleanor had come in. Karen and Eleanor had very few words to say to each other after that incident. Eleanor thought that a few days would pass and Karen's anger would subside. But Karen's anger grew into a deep-seated resentment and that resentment soon turned to hatred—a hatred that has festered for ten years.

When we are blinded by hatred, it is almost impossible to see our own sin.

Eleanor and Karen both have families now, and yet the sting of what happened ten years ago has not lessened. They still avoid each other at church functions and do not work together on committees. A few of us friends have tried to act as mediators down through the years in an attempt to bring them together—without success. Perhaps the wounds are too deep. The saddest part of this entire situation is watching the "spill-over" into the lives of Eleanor's and Karen's children. The children reflect the animosity the parents have for each other. This entire situation continues to invade the otherwise beautiful fellowship at our church. Where and when will the hatred end?

The Life Lesson

But if ye bite and devour one another, take heed that ye be not consumed one of another (Galatians 5:15).

Carrying hatred and malice toward someone in your heart can be as deadly as injecting poison into your body on a daily basis. Such a deadly injection into the physical body ensures rapid physical deterioration. Likewise, a daily dose of hatred and bitterness that you may harbor in your spirit ensures a rapid spiritual deterioration.

We have all been offended by someone sometime in our lives. When we do not go to our offender, express our feelings, and seek reconciliation, our resentment over the offense can turn to bitterness, and bitterness can turn to hatred. Hatred can eat away at the fiber of one's being much like a cancer eats away at the bones. The feeling of hatred can cause a physical reaction in the body. Deepseated resentment of others often manifests itself in feelings of anxiety, uneasiness, apprehension, and worry. The stomach reacts by producing excess acid. You might experience a headache or nervousness. Many old folks will tell you that hating others can actually make you sick and more susceptible to disease and infection.

Christianity is a religion of the heart; outward compliance alone is not enough. Bitterness against someone who has wronged you is an evil cancer within you and will eventually destroy you. Don't allow a "root of bitterness" to grow inside you.

Follow peace with all men…looking diligently lest any man fail of the grace of God; lest any root of bitterness springing up trouble you, and thereby many be defiled (Hebrews 12:14-15).

Hatred and bitterness are like weeds with long roots that grow in the heart and corrupt all of life. When we are blinded by hatred, it is almost impossible to see our own sin. Like a small root that grows into a great tree, bitterness springs up in our hearts and overshadows even our deepest Christian relationship. Bitterness brings with it jealousy, dissension, and immorality. When the Holy Spirit fills our lives, there is no room for bitterness.

When we are not motivated by love, we become critical of others. We stop looking for good in them and see only their faults. Soon the unity of believers is broken. Have you said negative things about people behind their back? Have you focused on others' shortcomings instead of their strengths? Remind yourself of Jesus' command to love others as we love ourselves.

Thou shalt love thy neighbor as thyself (Matthew 22:39b).

When you begin to feel critical of someone:

- Make a mental list of that person's positive qualities.

- Don't say anything behind someone's back that you wouldn't say to her face.
- Know that God is listening.

Christians get plenty of hatred from the world. Therefore, we need love and support from each other. Jesus said not to be surprised if the world hates, because it hated Him.

If the world hate you, ye know that it hated Me before it hated you (John 15:18).

Do you allow small problems and disagreements to get in the way of loving other believers? We are to love one another as Jesus loved us, and He loved us enough to give His life for us. We may not have to die for someone, but there are other ways that we can demonstrate our sacrificial love for others: listening, helping, encouraging, supporting, giving. Think of someone in particular who needs this kind of love today. Give her all the love and positive feedback you can, and then try to give a little more. Pray this prayer:

Lord, examine my heart. If there is any root of bitterness in me, I ask that You remove it. I want the love of God to shine clearly in my life. Heal my heart of the pain of offenses against me. Help me to love others as Christ has loved me.

Everyone must enroll in the "school of forgiveness." It is a required course. Hating others requires our time, energy, and focus. It is stress-producing. Stress is inevitable; stress-related illness is not. Hatred and anger are constant companions. Anger is an emotion that will not allow you to live if you carry it around over a long period of time. Learn to love others as Christ has loved you— even when you were "unlovable." There are three things you can do to begin to accomplish this:

1. Be easy. Be a comfortable sort of person so that there is no strain in being with you. Being with you should make people feel better.

2. Don't *react*. Avoid being on edge and sensitive so that you are easily hurt. People instinctively shy away from the super-sensitive for fear of arousing an unpleasant reaction.

3. Heal. Sincerely attempt to heal, on an honest basis, every misunderstanding that you may have with others. Mentally and physically drain off your grievances and maintain an attitude of good will toward everyone.

A Tidbit of Wisdom

Some people are always grumbling because roses have thorns; I am thankful that thorns have roses. No one is perfect.

Story 5—Overcoming Obstacles

The Story

The happiest people don't necessarily have the best of everything. They just make the best of everything.

Barbara had a look of sheer terror on her face while she shared her "tale of woe" with her best friend Marva. Barbara was desperate. Her dream world and fairy-tale existence seemed to be crashing down around her, all within a week's time. She leaned back in her kitchen chair to provide more "breathing room" for herself and the child she and her husband Charles were expecting in four months. "When trouble comes, it comes in three's," Barbara explained.

Charles just lost his job as a result of downsizing at his company. They both worried about how they would provide for the child that was on the way. Barbara and Charles had only been married for a year when God answered their prayers for a child of their own. Barbara also had a five-year-old son from a previous marriage.

As a young widow, Barbara had struggled to raise her child on her own as a single parent. Charles was a blessing from the Lord. He was a good man, who worked hard and loved God. The news of Charles' job loss was a crushing blow, but Charles and Barbara were people of faith and Charles was a smart man. Both knew it was only a matter of time and prayer before he found new employment.

Barbara could handle the bad news of the job loss, but she could not handle the chilling news she had received from her doctor earlier that afternoon. Barbara's test results showed that she was in the early stages of multiple sclerosis, a degenerative nerve disease. What she thought were twinges and the aches and pains of a growing baby had been the harbingers of a physical condition that had the potential of making her an invalid or ultimately destroying her life.

Barbara wanted to die to escape her troubles. Job loss, financial devastation, and disease were gross interruptions in her goals and plans for life. "How does a person cope with all of this? Why did God allow this to happen to me?" she asked Marva with a look of desperation on her face.

The Life Lesson

Greater is He that is in you, than he that is in the world (1 John 4:4b).

Obstacles are those frightful things you see when you take your eyes off the goal.

In a moment of desperation and discouragement, King David said:

...Oh that I had wings like a dove! for then would I fly away, and be at rest. ... I would hasten my escape from the windy storm and tempest (Psalm 55:6,8).

David wanted to "get away from it all," but we do not criticize him for honestly expressing his despair and wanting to escape from his troubles. All of us have shared these same feelings at one time or another. But we have also learned that we cannot run away from life's burdens and problems.

When we find ourselves facing obstacles and difficult situations, many of us pray, "God, get me out of this!" If nothing happens immediately, then we pray, "God, when will I get out of this?" But what we ought to be praying is, "God, what should I get out of this?" There is a purpose in trials and problems. God does not cause problems to occur in our lives, nor does He plant obstacles in our way to keep us from reaching our goals and experiencing personal happiness. Rather God often removes the hedge of protection from around His people in order to teach us valuable spiritual lessons. Obstacles can be excellent teachers of spiritual lessons that we could learn no other way.

A Tidbit of Wisdom

No obstacle can crush you. Every obstacle yields to stern resolve. Experience is not only what happens to you, but it is what you *do* with what happens to you.

Story 6—Victory Over Suffering

The Story

Pain is inevitable. Suffering is optional.

George and Denise came to my office angry and bitter over the death of their only child. The death of their four-month-old was even more tragic because he was an adopted child. George and Denise had tried to have a child for 12 years. After trying everything, they contacted an adoption agency and waited another two years before a healthy African-American baby boy was available. They felt that God had finally smiled on them. Baby George, Jr., was their long-awaited answer to prayer. Now, at four months of age, he lost his life to SIDS (Sudden Infant Death Syndrome).

This couple had actually come to my office to tell me that they had given up on God. "God has turned His back on us," George said, "so now we are turning our backs on Him." Strangely enough, I understood their anger. They were fine, upstanding members of our church and community. They did not deserve this suffering. There were many other parents who were much less loving and responsible as parents. As a pastor I did what I knew to do best, I turned to the Word of God for answers.

The Life Lesson

But He knoweth the way I take: when He hath tried me, I shall come forth as gold (Job 23:10).

At one time or another, everyone must go through experiences of trial and testing. This is one of the facts of life that we must accept if we intend to make circumstances our servants and not our masters. None of us enjoy pain. Pain is not something that we pray for or eagerly anticipate, but sometimes we need it.

Next to our Lord Jesus Christ, perhaps no person mentioned in the Bible suffered more than Job. First he lost his wealth, then his children, then his health, and then the encouragement and support of his wife and his friends. Job sat alone on his ash heap, listening to his friends falsely diagnose his case and try to prove that he was a secret sinner who was being punished by God. Their theory, of course, was that God always blesses the righteous with health and wealth but punishes the wicked by making them suffer.

God does sometimes use physical suffering to discipline His children. But this does not mean that every case of suffering in the family of God is necessarily a punishment from God. It may be that God has other purposes in mind when He permits us to go into the fiery furnace of pain. Joseph suffered in various ways for 13 years, yet he was certainly not suffering because of disobedience to God. The prophet Jeremiah and the apostle Paul both suffered greatly, yet their suffering came because they obeyed God, not because they disobeyed Him. Job understood the fiery furnace of pain. God was purging away the dross so that Job might come out of the furnace as pure gold.

The furnace is one of the most vivid images of testing and trials found in Scripture. Just as silver and gold are purified by fire, so the Lord purifies the hearts of men by fiery trials. It takes intense heat to purify gold and silver. Similarly, it often takes the heat of trials for Christians to be purified. Through trials, God shows us what is in us and clears out anything that gets in the way of complete trust in Him.

The [re]*fining pot is for silver, and the furnace for gold: but the Lord trieth the hearts* (Proverbs 17:3).

Wealthy Solomon knew something about gold and silver, but he also knew something about life. He knew that God sometimes allows His people to be put into the fiery furnace of suffering in order to prove them and to purify them.

Peter says, "If your faith remains strong after being tried in the test tube of fiery trials, it will bring you much praise."

That the trial of your faith, being much more precious than of gold that perisheth, though it be tried with fire, might be found unto praise and honour and glory at the appearing of Jesus Christ (1 Peter 1:7).

As gold is heated, impurities float to the top and can be skimmed off. Steel is tempered or strengthened by being heated in fire. Likewise, our trials, struggles, and problems strengthen our faith and make us useful to God. Job understood this principle. Like Job, we must enter the furnace of faith and trust the Father to accomplish His purposes in our life. It is better to go through the furnace and come out as pure gold than to be too cheap to be useful in the hands of the Father.

A Tidbit of Wisdom

Give me a task too big, too hard for human hands; then I shall come at last to lean on Thee, and in leaning, find my strength.

Story 7 — Handling Change

The Story

We change when the misery of where we are is greater than the fear of change.

"I could feel it in every inch and ounce of my five-foot, six-inch frame. I could see it in every mirror and plate glass window. Each reflection offered a painful reminder of how unhealthy I had become. I could hear it when I wheezed as I climbed the stairs to my house; each labored breath mimicked the creak of a rusty hinge."

These were the words of a close friend as we sat at her kitchen table. Charlotte weighed well over 300 pounds. She always moaned and groaned about her weight. She often cried and complained while shoveling down junk food and soft drinks. The more depressed she became about her weight, the more she ate.

Charlotte's life was completely out of control and she knew it. She was always ready to blame a myriad of problems and other people for her weight gain. I would just listen as a good friend ought while growing increasingly weary of the constant blaming and complaining. Charlotte was stuck in a place where she knew she had to change her life, but her desire was not deep enough to motivate her to put that desire in action.

In other areas of her life, Charlotte seemed like a tower of strength. She was strong and intelligent and had a personal relationship with the Lord. So why couldn't she gain control over this area of her life? She had so many goals and desires and good things she wanted for herself. Even the desire to change her lifestyle and eating habits was there. She talked about it all the time, but she seemed to do very little to bring about that change.

One day, we were discussing relationships. Charlotte spoke with much pain and anguish in her voice. She spoke of the constant disappointment she experienced as a result of numerous broken relationships and of the deep feelings of rejection and abandonment she felt. In her mind, Charlotte felt that the weight was protection against the attention of others, especially men, in her life and thus was a shield against possible rejection and hurt. The old adage, "It's not what you're eating but it's what's eating you" was so true in Charlotte's case. At the age of

45, she knew her situation would not change unless she made a conscious effort to do so. Fatigue followed her like a shadow. It was no longer an issue of vanity. It was a matter of survival. "My bulging belly, pudgy toes, and D-cup, 'spilleth over' bosom are symptoms of a bigger problem," Charlotte said. "It is time for a change, time to get healthy."

The Life Lesson

For I know the thoughts that I think toward you, saith the Lord, thoughts of peace, and not of evil, to give you an expected end (Jeremiah 29:11).

Most of us know that positive life changes do not come easily. We all face a battle any time we enter the process of change. A battle rages during the process of grabbing for the new while giving up—yet still hanging on to—the old and familiar. To win this battle, change must be an *inside-out* affair, starting with acknowledgment of the problem and ending with the Problem Solver, God. Ultimately, God is the genuine transformer of our lives.

If you seek God first in every challenging situation, you will not see change as a threat but as an opportunity to let God work in new ways. The first and biggest step in the challenge of change is recognizing the need for change and passionately desiring it. The desire to change must rise up to face the fear of change. Newness and change give opportunity for the devil to stir old areas of fear within us. Acknowledging that this is a natural reaction is important. Denying the threat of the new will keep you stuck in the old. Once a person recognizes the need for change and passionately desires it, she must:

- Look to God for His power.
- Let go of destructive behavior patterns.
- Receive God's healing and restoration.
- Receive God's gift.

Look To God For His Power

Fear of change is a natural feeling, but the natural loses its strength in the face of the supernatural, transforming power of God. We must look to God for His power. The same power that raised Jesus from the dead is resident in those of us who are believers. Jesus went to the cross so that through His redeeming grace we could have victory in situations that challenge us. God's power is available to renew and transform us if we will choose to open up our comfort zone and surrender.

Habits and thought patterns developed over a lifetime are battle-resistant to change and do not give up easily. They require Holy Spirit power and patience to be unlearned. Make it a goal to seek God daily for strength to get through that day—and sometimes that very hour. God eagerly awaits our petitions and is faithful to meet our every need.

Let Go of Destructive Behavior Patterns

Letting go is an important step in bringing about change in one's life. We must make room for the new in our lives. We must let go of destructive behavior patterns that interfere with our enjoyment of life. Solomon in his wisdom wrote:

There is a time for everything, and a season... (Ecclesiastes 3:1 NIV).

There is not room enough within you for both old patterns and new ones. In every transition, happy or sad, we must let go of what *was*. Until we do, we cannot appreciate what *is*. Releasing the "former things" is a process, not an event. Allow yourself time to adjust emotionally.

Receive God's Healing and Restoration

With God's healing and restoration, you can walk in a new reality made from the fragments of your former life. Have you ever dropped a piece of glass and watched it shatter into tiny pieces? Our lives are much like those broken fragments. Now picture in your mind a beautiful stained-glass window—a work of art made of pieces of broken glass, yet complete and marvelous to behold. This is what Christ can make of the broken pieces of your life.

Learn to process your feelings in the light of Jesus Christ. Look at yourself and your feelings with candor, and lift them up to the Lord for His perspective and healing touch. Keep a journal. This will help you identify otherwise vague feelings of anxiety.

Receive God's Gift

Remember that satan will sow seeds of hopelessness in your mind. His voice says, "You can never change. Look at the life that you've had, what you've done, and what's been done to you." Satan seeks to steal our hope and self-worth and strives to destroy the work of God in us. But God speaks truth into our life. His voice says that you have been created to be a mighty overcomer, that you are loved, that you need only receive His gift and trust Him.

The road to change is laden with potholes and many unexpected twists and turns. It is easy to lose your footing or get lost along the way. The average person will make several tries before she eventually succeeds. Most former smokers, for example, report three to four serious attempts before they finally kick the habit. Most people typically make New Year's resolutions for at least five consecutive years before the promises finally take hold. But it doesn't have to take that long. You will be better able to negotiate the obstacles in your path and reach your goals if you understand the stages of change people pass through on their way to ultimate success.

Understand That You Are Not a Failure

Stop kicking yourself. Many people continue to indulge in high-risk or unhealthy behaviors despite pleas or warnings to stop. Take heart, you are not a failure. Unresponsiveness and even giant steps backward may actually be advances down the road to change. Lifestyle changes occur incrementally. When major lifestyle changes are made, we move through six clearly defined stages: precontemplation, contemplation, preparation, action, maintenance, and termination.

In the precontemplation stage, people will deny a problem exists or blame their genetic makeup, family, or other external factors for their weight that is getting out of control. For example, instead of facing up to the problem when it was manageable, this person will avoid the bathroom scale and wear fashionably baggy clothes that hide the flab. Contemplators recognize the problem, try to understand it, and begin to make plans to alter their behavior. The preparation stage involves setting a date for action and publicly announcing the intended behavioral change. The action level requires the greatest amount of time, energy, and commitment. In this phase you can "see something happening." Once the goal is achieved you reach the maintenance stage, a time when you must struggle to avoid lapses and relapses. This period can last anywhere from six months to a lifetime, depending on the problem. The final, or termination, stage is the time when the temptation no longer exists and a person exits the cycle of change.

A Tidbit of Wisdom

Food and heartache are intertwined.

Story 8—Making the Best of Single Parenting

The Story

Your children learn more of your faith during
the bad times than they do during the good times.

Millicent's Story

Single parent! The words themselves frightened me beyond belief. I am not sure why. I had known many other women who were mother and father to their children. Somehow I never thought I would be one, though. Most of the women I knew had husbands who had abandoned them and did not financially support their children. This made single motherhood especially difficult. As a result, most of these single mothers were forced to work long hours outside of the home doing a job that took them away from the most important job of all—motherhood.

I was especially horrified about my new single parent status because I had planned and prepared to be an excellent parent for so many years. I was glad that I had completed my education and enjoyed a wonderful career first so that when I married and started a family, I could devote my time and attention to building a stable home and raising healthy, productive youngsters. I had watched many girlfriends struggle as they worked full-time inside and outside of the home while also trying to fulfill their role as a wife and mother. They were always burned out. I had determined that would not be me. I would make sure that I had time to nurture my children properly.

When I first became a single parent, fear consumed me. But the initial shock wore off quickly because I had two children—a boy and a girl just out of diapers—no child support, a home to maintain, and a life to live. I shared my fears with a trusted friend. "How can I do this?" I said bewildered. Then my friend said something that jolted me back to reality and started me on a plan to survive and overcome my fears. "You've always been a single parent," she said, "and you've done a fine job to this point." She was right. For several years I had already been both mother and father, not by choice, but by necessity. Now divorced, my singleness as a parent was official. All I had to do was look around me for the help I needed, sent directly from God, to continue to do what I was already successfully doing to parent my children.

The Life Lesson

Lo, children are an heritage from the Lord (Psalm 127:3a).

The two most difficult aspects of single parenting is the overwhelming feeling of "aloneness" and the "fear of failure." Parenting is a full-time and sometimes overwhelming job for two parents with a healthy marriage. Facing the world as a single parent, in addition to coping with the death of a marriage, is probably one of the most devastating of human crises. Many times depression comes from the feeling of being in this thing alone. The prophet Elijah hid under a tree in a state of depression over what he had lost. Later, he ended up in a cave wishing he were dead simply because he thought he was going through a crisis alone.

> *But he himself went a day's journey into the wilderness, and came and sat down under a juniper tree: and he requested for himself that he might die; and said, It is enough: Now ,O Lord, take away my life: for I am not better than my fathers* (1 Kings 19:4).

Elijah felt alienated. He was functioning under the misguided notion that he was left alone. Elijah failed to look outside of his sphere and realize that God never leaves anyone alone. God's Word promises that believers never have to fear "aloneness" in any situation. The Lord has said,

> *...I will never leave thee nor forsake thee* (Hebrews 13:5).

When I began to look at the women around me—in my own extended family, my church, and my community—I discovered many, many women who through no fault of their own found themselves facing the world as single parents. Many of them raised children who have become fine, productive citizens.

I had the opportunity to meet Mrs. Coretta Scott King, the widow of the slain Civil Rights leader, Dr. Martin Luther King, Jr. When we think of Mrs. King, we think of a woman of grace, intelligence, and stamina—and she is a single parent. After the untimely assassination of her husband, she was also thrust into the world of single parenthood as a young woman facing the world with four young children. In spite of the challenges of single parenting, Coretta King raised four talented, well-educated, Christ-centered children. And I determined that if she could do it, so could I. Despite the challenges, anyone can be a successful parent, whether one is handling the job alone or with a reliable partner. The following items can work to ensure that success:

1. Get a support network.
2. Allow God to work in mysterious ways.
3. Open your heart to God's plan for your life.

Get a Support Network

No one can truly succeed in any endeavor without the help of others. You must understand that God has help available for you, and it is all around you. God's help may not come through the traditional help of a spouse, but there are surrogate fathers and mothers in your extended family, church, and community, persons whose wisdom and love can mend the breach of the empty void with your children. Don't be afraid to reach out and ask others for help. Other people, especially those who have raised children, understand the weight of the task and privilege of guiding a child through life. More likely than not, they are waiting for an opportunity to assist.

Allow God to Work in Mysterious Ways

Many times when help does not come from the source we expect, we give up as if God is limited to just one channel of expression. God is very diverse. God has many ways to give help, encouragement, and support to His people. Be open to allow God to bless you with the help you need from unexpected sources.

Open Your Heart to God's Plan for Your Life

God always has a plan for our lives. Many times we do not see how difficult circumstances can work in a positive way to carry out God's overall plan for us. But God does not see our lives as a series of episodes. God sees the bigger picture of what Christlike characteristics He wants to build in us through the challenges we face. Every difficult situation is ultimately designed to bless us. Never allow depression to blind you from seeing an opportunity that God created or has allowed to bless you. Unnecessary bitterness can be eradicated if you will open your heart to the plans of God. The Lord has many ways with which He can meet your needs. God provides for His own. He will cause people to want to bless you. He will provide someone who will not mind helping you through a tough time. It may be someone who will babysit for your children, or He may send someone your way with an unexpected material blessing such as groceries or money. Thank God that He has people whom He will use to bless you so that you will be able to survive the challenges you face.

A Tidbit of Wisdom

Parents are just babysitters for God.

Story 9—Coping with Death

The Story

When you are lonely, cultivate the companionship of the "Great Friend."

Sheila's Story

I mourned my husband's death, but I did not cry. I couldn't. If I were to give death that kind of emotional rein, I would go crazy. You protect the part of yourself that is hurting in the best way you know how—by fighting or closing yourself off—however you work it out.

My husband was a very private person. We were only married for 12 years when he found out that he had a brain tumor. He made me promise to tell no one. His illness was a secret nightmare that we both shared. My husband could be generous and compassionate, but he could also be very protective and *all wall*. He had a brain tumor for five years. It was not until he died that many people even knew that he was sick.

My husband fought his illness alone. Every day I looked for signs of physical and emotional deterioration. He waged war in a battle as a lone soldier. He shut everyone out, and I resented him for that. But now I find myself doing the same thing. It has been almost two years since my husband died, and even though there is not a day that goes by that I do not think about him, I cannot cry. I have tried, but the tears are bottled up somewhere. If I could break through my own wall, I think I would feel better and could get on with my life.

Everyone compliments me about how strong I am. But my perceived strength is only a cover-up for the utter helplessness I feel against something over which I have no control. I am so frozen in grief that I find it hard to pray. Praying is something my husband and I did every evening before retiring. My husband was a saved man who loved God as I do. Right now, I find it difficult to pray to a God who would allow this much pain to touch my life.

The Life Lesson

Precious in the sight of the Lord is the death of His saints (Psalm 116:15).

When someone close to us dies, we need a long period of time to work through our grief. Crying and sharing our feelings with others helps us recover and go on with life. Allow yourself and others the freedom to grieve over the loss of a loved one and a long enough time to bring grieving to completion.

As said before, death casts a frightening shadow over our lives because we are the most helpless in its presence. The only person who can take us through the valley of death and bring us to the other side is the God of life, our Shepherd. In Psalm 23, God is portrayed as a caring shepherd and a dependable guide. Because the Lord is our Shepherd, we have everything we need, even space and comfort in times of overwhelming grief.

The Lord is my shepherd; I shall not want (Psalm 23:1).

There are joys and benefits of a life lived in companionship with God. We can enjoy these benefits now and eternally. God does not exempt believers from the day-to-day circumstances of life. Believers and unbelievers alike experience pain, trouble, death, and failure at times.

For He maketh His sun to rise on the evil and on the good, and sendeth rain on the just and on the unjust (Matthew 5:45b).

Believers have a security that unbelievers do not have. The unbeliever has a sense of hopelessness about life and confusion over his true purpose on earth. Those who seek after God, however, can move ahead confidently with what they know is right and important in God's eyes. David speaks about this unique sense of security felt by believers.

I have set the Lord always before me: because He is at my right hand, I shall not be moved (Psalm 16:8).

For many, death is a darkened door at the end of their lives, a passageway to an unknown and feared destiny. But for God's people, death is a bright doorway to a new and better life. So why do we fear death? Is it because of the pain we expect, the separation from our loved ones, the surprise of it? God can help us deal with those fears. He has shown us that death is just another step in the continuing eternal life we began when we started to follow Him. Death is not final; it is the first step into eternity.

In the way of righteousness is life; and in the pathway thereof there is no death (Proverbs 12:28).

Paul said that both life and death are our servants. How can this be? While non-believers are victims of life, swept along by its current and wondering if there is meaning to it, believers use life well because they understand its true purpose. Non-believers can only fear death. For believers, however, death holds no terrors because Christ conquered them all.

Whether Paul, or Apollos, or Cephas, or the world, or life, or death, or things present, or things to come; all are yours (1 Corinthians 3:22).

Paul was not afraid to die because he was confident of spending eternity with Christ. Facing the unknown is cause for anxiety, and losing loved ones hurts deeply, but if we believe in Jesus Christ, we can share Paul's hope and confidence of eternal life in Christ.

A Tidbit of Wisdom

Life is like a coin. You can spend it any way you wish, but you can only spend it once.

Story 10—Overcoming a Life Crisis

The Story

People see God every day; they just don't recognize Him.

Jenny's Story

I had my life all mapped out. Phil and I had been married for only two years. I waited to marry because I wanted it to be right. I did not want to be a statistic on the ever-growing list of divorces. Phil was a good man, well-educated, a family man, hard-working, decent, everything a Christian woman like me wanted. Then a major crisis caused our fairy-tale lifestyle to come crashing down around us. Phil was diagnosed with ALS, or Lou Gerhig's disease, a degenerative nerve condition that weakens and finally kills its victim.

Phil and I had had troubles before, but nothing like this. While we were dating his mother had cancer, and she died an agonizing death just four months before our wedding. With much prayer and patience, we weathered that storm. Last year we experienced a miscarriage. Phil was very comforting and reassuring. We were told by the doctors that miscarriage is not uncommon, and since there was no indication of a serious problem, we would easily conceive a child again. We weathered that storm with God's help—but now this. How much can a person take? I vacillate between overwhelming despair and being just plain angry with God.

I have searched feverishly for answers. If I could just find a reason for this crisis, it would ease my conscience. Phil always took very good care of himself. He was somewhat of a fanatic when it came to exercise and diet. He did not smoke or drink alcohol. Yet this disease has trapped us in a way that we do not know how we got into it nor how we will get out. I admit that all this has made me bitter. I don't even pray for Phil's healing because somehow I don't think God is really listening. Such a prayer request seems foolish. I have read every book and article I could get my hands on about ALS. No one survives this crisis. How could a loving Father allow this to happen to His own children? There are many people who do not love God as I do, and yet they are not facing what I am going through. It all seems so unfair.

The Life Lesson

Casting all your care upon Him: for He careth for you (1 Peter 5:7).

Many times it is only through repeated experience that we learn that God is able to provide for us. God has preserved many examples in Scripture so that we can learn to trust Him the first time. By focusing on God's faithfulness in the past we can avoid responding to crisis with fear and complaining. God gave the Israelites a pillar of cloud and fire so they would know that God was with them on their journey to the Promised Land day and night. Even though they encountered peril, and even unknown danger, the constant reminder of God's presence was comforting. God has given us His Word—something the Israelites did not have—so that we can have the same assurance.

And the Lord went before them by day in a pillar of a cloud, to lead them the way; and by night in a pillar of fire, to give them light, to go by day and night (Exodus 13:21).

As the Israelites looked to the pillar of cloud and fire, we can look to God's Word day and night to know that He is with us and helping us on our journey.

Trapped against the Red Sea, the Israelites faced the Egyptian army, which was sweeping in for the kill. The Israelites thought they were doomed. After watching God's powerful hand deliver them from bondage in Egypt, their only response was fear, whining, and despair. Evidently they forgot how God had brought them through a hopeless situation just days before. Their lack of faith in God is startling. Yet how often do we find ourselves doing the same thing—grumbling and complaining over situations instead of remembering what God has done and drawing upon the knowledge we already have of what God is able to do for us. Moses had a positive attitude.

And Moses said unto the people, Fear ye not, stand still, and see the salvation of the Lord, which He will show to you to day: for the Egyptians whom ye have seen today, ye shall see them again no more for ever (Exodus 14:13).

The people were hostile and despairing, but Moses encouraged them to watch the wonderful way God would rescue them. When it looked as if they were trapped, Moses called upon God to intervene. We may not be chased by an army, but we may still feel trapped. Although our first reaction could be despair, we should adopt the attitude of "watch and see what God will do."

When a crisis strikes our life, we may not know the reason. It may be the result of our own disobedience, the result of someone else's sin, or the result of natural disaster. Since we don't know, we are to search our hearts to see if we are at peace with God. God's Spirit will, like a great searchlight, reveal those areas we need to deal with.

Since calamity and crisis are not always the result of wrongdoing, we must guard against assigning or accepting blame for every tragedy we encounter. Misplaced guilt is one of satan's favorite weapons against believers. How we react to crisis in our lives reflects what we believe. Paul looked for opportunities to demonstrate his faith when he faced bad situations. Paul was imprisoned in Rome. Imprisonment would cause many people to become bitter and cold or to give up. But Paul saw it as one more opportunity to spread the good news of Jesus Christ. Paul realized that his current circumstances were not as important as what he did with them.

But I would ye should understand, brethren, that the things which happened unto me have fallen out rather unto the furtherance of the gospel (Philippians 1:12).

Turning a bad situation into a good one, Paul reached out to the Roman soldiers and encouraged those Christians who were afraid of persecution. We may not be in a literal prison, but we still have many times in which we may become discouraged by crisis in our lives, including times of indecision, financial burden, family conflict, church conflict, or job loss. How we react in such situations reflects what we believe. Whether or not the situation improves, your faith will grow stronger.

A Tidbit of Wisdom

Give your troubles to God; He will be up all night anyway.

Story 11—Remarriage and Family-Blending

The Story

It's not whether you get knocked down; it's whether you get up.

Glenda's Story

Mike and I are on the verge of ending our marriage. I could understand it if the reason centered around infidelity or some basic incompatibility. But our issues center around the children. Mike and I are both single parents. Mike was never married to his children's mother. His children are teenagers who live in another state with their mother, and my three elementary school-age children live with us. We knew going into the marriage that a blended family would be a challenge, but we were not aware of the unique problems we would confront almost every day.

Mike is a strict disciplinarian who wants to run our home like an army boot camp. He says that this type of parenting worked with him and he also raised his own children this way. I've said to him, "If this type of child-rearing works, then why do your teenage children dread coming to spend time with you?" Since making that statement, my husband has almost completely shut down. He won't even discuss the subject. My children sense the tension and sometimes use it to manipulate us. I want my children to love my husband as I do. He is such a wonderful man. I don't know why they can't see that.

My husband's children don't like me either. I suspect that their mother is the reason for that. She is always very brief and abrupt when I talk with her on the phone. I am not her enemy. It seems to me that it would be in her best interest and in the interest of everyone involved for us to work hard at getting along as a family. But that seems like an impossible wish. My husband does not help either. I've asked him to talk with her and call a truce for the sake of the sanity of the family, but he does not seem to hear me. My husband and I have only been married for two years, and I do not see how we will survive for two more years if this family situation does not improve.

I thought love "the second time around" was supposed to be "sweeter." Whoever coined that phrase was obviously not involved in a second marriage. Somehow I thought I "had it right" this time. After all, I do have 15 years experience under my belt in this thing called marriage—and the wounds and battle scars to prove it. I thought this would be easier because I'm older, more settled, more in touch with myself, more aware of who I am. In other words, I feel that I am bringing more to the table than I did when I first married at age 19. I didn't know what I was getting myself into. It just seemed like the right thing to do at the time.

I enjoyed being single so much that I vowed to never take "the plunge" again. Now after enjoying almost ten years of freedom and independence I find myself married again. Mike is a wonderful man. This is his first marriage, and my second. I think he has a more idealized concept of what marriage is like, because he has no frame of reference to draw upon— only what he sees on TV or reads in romance novels. Before we were married, I told Mike that marriage is "a work in progress." In other words, the marriage we have the first year will not be the marriage we have in two years or five years or ten. Hopefully, our relationship will change and grow over time. All this takes work and time and effort. Mike doesn't seem to want to do "the work." He thinks our marriage should just happen because we're "in love." Becoming one is much more difficult than I ever imagined.

Mike and I struggled when we were dating because I was a divorced woman. So many people told him that he could "do better." The ridicule caused us to find another church where we would feel supported as a couple. I never want it said that "we couldn't make it" or "I told you so." Still, this has been a very difficult two years.

The Life Lesson

Marriage is honourable in all... (Hebrews 13:4).

The myth of falling in love and living happily ever after (with ease, tranquility, riches, etc.) is as much wishful thinking in a second serious relationship as it was in the first one. We tend to handle our love relationships differently from other relationships we enter into—whether business or personal. We want romance and passion. Who wants to work at love? It's either happening or it's not. Love relationships are not easy. Even the happiest couples will admit to that. Unhappy couples, the embittered and the scorned, allow that reality to become an obstacle to happiness. And so when they hit rough times they run, strike out, cheat...and then they vow, "Never again."

Successful married couples have the same problems as unsuccessful couples. The ones who succeed in their relationships, however, treat problems as challenges and not obstacles. They realize that love is always a "work in progress." Couples who are involved in a second or third marriage must carefully examine their earlier mistakes in matters of the heart to guard against their history repeating itself.

The union of husband and wife merges two persons in such a way that little can affect one without also affecting the other. Oneness in marriage does not mean losing your personality in the personality of the other. Instead, it means caring for your spouse as you care for yourself, learning to anticipate the other person's needs, helping the other person become all he or she can be. The creation story tells of God's plan that husband and wife should be one:

And they shall be one flesh (Genesis 2:24b).

Jesus also referred to this plan:

...For this cause shall a man leave father and mother, and shall cleave to his wife: and they twain shall be one flesh? (Matthew 19:5)

Concerning the issue of remarriage, God's capacity for restoring life is beyond our understanding. Forests burn down and are able to grow back. Broken bones heal. Even grief is not a permanent condition. Married people who find themselves alone as a result of divorce or death can find love and happiness again in a Christ-centered marriage. God is able to bring good out of tragedy. The key to contentment in marriage is a solid foundation based upon God's Word and an intimate relationship with Him. Don't make the mistake of leaving God out of your marriage. If you do, the foundation will be shaky and the futility of working to become "one" will cause it to crumble.

Except the Lord build the house, they labour in vain that build it:except the Lord keep the ciy, the watchman waketh but in vain (Psalm 127:1).

Married couples establish homes and sentries guard cites, but both these activities are futile unless God is with them. A family without God can never experience the spiritual bond that God brings to relationships. A city without God will crumble from evil and corruption on the inside. Likewise, any marriage without God is a disaster waiting to happen.

Submission is a key element in the smooth functioning of any business, government, or family. No one ever talks about the need for a man to submit to his wife. But if more husbands understood this principle from God's Word, there would be less strife and need for control in relationships. It is essential to understand that submission is not surrender, withdrawal, or apathy. Submission does not mean inferiority either, because God created all people in His image and all have equal value. Submission is mutual commitment and cooperation. Thus, God calls for submission by choice, not force. Paul counseled all believers to submit to one another by choice—husbands to wives, and wives to husbands.

Submitting yourselves one to another in the fear of God (Ephesians 5:21).

Marriage is a holy union, a living symbol, a precious relationship that needs tender, self-sacrificing care. The following points should be kept in mind when "building" a strong maritial relationship:

- Keep talking (communication is vital).
- Be patient (understand that we all bring baggage from previous relationships into our marriage).
- Pray, pray, pray—together.

Make God your highest priority, and let Him do the building. To strengthen the bond in your marriage, pray this prayer:

Lord, we thank You for love and marriage. Bless our union as husband and wife. Help us know that we are Your gift to each other. We know that love starts with You because You are love. Teach us to work together to build our relationship upon You and Your Word. Grant us patience and unconditional love for each other. Let our relationship reflect Christ. Amen.

A Tidbit of Wisdom

A marriage may be made in Heaven, but the maintenance must be done on earth.

Story 12—Healing After Divorce

The Story

An error doesn't become a mistake until you refuse to correct it.

Cheryl's Story

I was raised in the church. My father was a deacon for 43 years before he died, and my mother still serves as a missionary at our home church. My parents enjoyed what seemed like a happy marriage for almost 60 years. That's why I can't believe that I am going through a divorce. I had what seemed to be the perfect role model for what to do to make a marriage work. And yet, with all my hard work and effort, I still found myself in family court listening to lawyers go back and forth as I tried to get financial support for our three school-age children. What hurts me most is that I am divorcing a man who vowed before God and 500 of our friends and relatives to love and honor me forever.

I've already been told by the ladies whom I work with in our church that there are certain areas of the ministry in which I can no longer serve because I will soon be a divorced woman.

I lived with guilt and condemnation for years before I made my decision to end my marriage. I was convinced that I would surely go to hell and that God would see to it that I was never in a happy relationship with a man again because of what I was about to do.

I have not shared my story with anyone. I don't need to have others score me on my level of misery to determine whether or not divorcing my husband is justified. After attending the funeral of my good friend Pat last year, I finally decided that that would not be me. Pat died of AIDS. She contracted the virus from her husband who was having an affair with another woman. I watched her agony as she wasted away to nothing. Her greatest source of pain was knowing that she would leave two young children without a mother to raise them. *And how does God get glory out of that?* I thought. It was only a week before her death as I visited her in the intensive care unit of the city hospital that she told me what she had and how she had contracted the HIV virus. I took what she said as God's warning to me.

My husband Warren has been seeing another woman for what I believe to be two years now. She is an old girlfriend who has relocated back to our town to be near him. I tried to tell myself that this affair was not happening. I drowned myself in denial until he stayed out all night one time last summer, and our oldest son saw him coming out of one of the local hotels with her. He does not want a divorce because he says "everybody makes one mistake" and that we are too "financially involved" to go through the hassle of divorce. But he wants to have his cake and eat it too. The affair has not stopped.

I have searched the Scriptures. My pastor told me that if a man wants to keep the marriage, then a wife is obligated to remain in the marriage. If this is what Scripture means, then what is marriage? I have learned that a husband can abandon his wife and still remain physically in the home. It seems to me that this makes a mockery of what God intended marriage to be. A couple can pass each other in their own home and still not speak to each other for days at a time. I know that if I remain in this arrangement my husband calls marriage, I will die like my friend Pat. My husband refuses to go to counseling. He won't pray with me about the situation, and He says that God does not dictate how he is to live his life. I've come to the conclusion that if I don't do something to save my life and the lives of my children, I won't have a life to think about.

The Life Lesson

A brother or a sister is not under bondage...God has called us to peace (1 Corinthians 7:15b)

Divorce seems to be epidemic in our society. Many of us have visited that loathsome place against our will and against our good judgment. So much in our society works against the preservation of marriage and the family. Paul addresses divorce in his letter to the believers at Corinth. Because of their desire to serve Christ, some people in the Corinthian church thought they ought to divorce their pagan spouses and marry Christians. However, Paul affirmed the marriage commitment. God's ideal of marriage is to stay together—ven when one spouse is not a believer. The Christian spouse should try to win the other to Christ.

For the unbelieving husband is sanctified by the wife, and the unbelieving wife is sanctified by the husband... (1 Corinthians 7:14).

It would be easy to rationalize leaving; however, Paul makes a strong case for staying with the unbelieving spouse and being a positive influence on the marriage. Then Paul goes on to say,

But if the unbelieving depart, let him depart. A brother or a sister is not under bondage in such cases: but God hath called us to peace (1 Corinthians 7:15).

Here we have a legal and scriptural reason for divorce and remarriage. If the unbeliever refuses to live with a wife or a husband because of Christianity, and if he or she is determined to leave on this account, the Christian is not under further marital bonds and should not be held responsible or punished by requirement to remain single the rest of his or her life because of the rebellion of another. The Christian is to submit to the breaking of the marriage covenant under such circumstances.

This verse is misused by some as a loophole to get out of marriage. But Paul's statements were given to encourage the Christian spouse to get along with the unbeliever and make the marriage work. If, however, the unbelieving spouse insists on leaving, Paul says to let him or her go. The only alternative would be to deny the faith to preserve the marriage. Divorce is as hurtful and destructive today as it was in Jesus' day. God intends marriage to be a lifetime commitment.

Therefore shall a man leave his father and his mother, and shall cleave unto his wife: and they shall be one flesh (Genesis 2:24).

When entering into a marriage, people should never consider divorce as an option for resolving problems. Jesus said that divorce is not permissible except if one's partner is unfaithful. This does not mean that divorce should automatically occur when a spouse commits adultery. Those who discover that their partner has been unfaithful should first attempt to forgive, reconcile, and restore the relationship. We are always to look for reasons to restore a relationship rather than for excuses to leave it. However, after the believer has done all that is required by God to restore the relationship and the unbelieving spouse still desires to abandon the marriage, then God blesses us as we go.

In an age of AIDS and other serious sexually transmitted diseases, the Christian must be wise concerning what the Scriptures say about the matters of infidelity and divorce. God is not glorified in the death of a spouse who foolishly remains with an unfaithful partner. God does receive glory when we prayerfully seek His guidance and direction in such painful situations. As you seek God's guidance and direction, use godly wisdom and do the following:

1. Get a good lawyer.
2. Follow through.
3. Protect your interests and those of your children.
4. Receive the blessings of God.

There are some positive sides to the painful aftermath of divorce. People who have been through a divorce do have substantial advantages in making love work later. They have a very real frame of reference when it comes to the commitment, energy, and rewards that always come up when people decide to be in a permanent relationship. They know all about relationships that don't work, and they have a special knowledge of the deadly behaviors and acts and attitudes that can ruin even a promising relationship. They have learned from past errors, and they now know how to focus on resolving conflicts. They have a stronger sense of commitment to their partner and relationship. They are committed to learning more about what makes relationships last, and usually they have found support systems that they can reach for when the going gets tough.

That is why people who are happily recoupled are a very special breed. Like decorated war heroes, they've been tested. Like the legendary phoenix, the bird that rises out of its ashes, they've been down and learned to fly again. They've learned to appreciate life and loved ones. As you weigh your options after divorce, it is important to see that with the pain also comes some positive things in your life. The first action that you should take is to write down all the positive changes that have occurred since your marriage ended. Make a list and be specific. For example, maybe you enjoy the chance to finally see the movie of your choice without criticism, even if it is a drippy tear-jerker. How about all the stuff that you don't feel obligated to enjoy anymore—like double-header baseball games, fishing trips, and out-of-control office parties? The possibilities are endless.

I recommend that you keep adding to the list and on days when you're feeling down about the divorce, take the list out and read it over. Even say to yourself, "I'm going to be all right. I'm going to get through this." The list is a technique to use when you are feeling overwhelmed or think that you are a failure for having "lost" at marriage. To calm your spirit during these stressful times, pray this prayer:

Lord, grant me peace that passes all understanding today. Help me know that You are aware of everything that I am experiencing and feeling. Allow the love of Christ to overshadow any feelings of failure and loneliness today. Help me to take one day at a time. Direct me as I rebuild my life. I release all bitterness and hurt. Today and everyday hereafter I will walk forward, never looking back, to enjoy the blessings You have for me. Amen.

A Tidbit of Wisdom

God does not do encores or repeat performances. Do a new thing. Don't try to revive what God wants to kill.

Story 13—Surviving Toxic Love

The Story

Love without esteem and respect cannot go far or reach high.
It is an angel with only one wing.

Jean's Story

I have been "in love" with Bill now for four years. Our relationship started out like most. We dated for a while and then began to spend most of our days together. I met Bill at work, so it was easy for us to see each other at lunch time and then spend our evenings together after work.

For me, it was love at first sight. Bill seemed perfect for me. He had all the qualities that I was looking for in a man. He was handsome, he dressed well, he was kind, he took me to nice places, and we shared many common interests. I knew Bill was a "good catch," so I knew I had to do something to make sure that I would be at the front of the line of all the other women who were attracted to him.

I knew Bill lived alone and had no other relatives in our town. He always talked about how he missed home and his mother's good cooking. So I decided to provide Bill with what he missed most. I planned it! I invited Bill over for a hot meal and a warm, homey atmosphere. I made myself irresistible.

I admit that Bill and I have not taken time to build a real friendship, but I have no time to waste. My biological clock has been ticking loudly for years. I figure we will become friends eventually—later. I have to get this relationship off the ground. For four years, I have put all my efforts into being and doing everything a man could ever want in a woman. Bill moved into my apartment; he drives my car; I buy most of the food and pay the utilities—he says he's saving for our future. I'm beginning to feel used. Bill says he loves me. It's just that I never knew that love hurt so deeply all the time.

I suspect that Bill is having another relationship. He's always unavailable for lunch now, and he's often late for dinner. Many nights during the week, he spends time with guy friends that I do not know. I've followed him and I check his pockets for phone numbers when he's asleep. Most days, I am consumed with anger. I've done everything that I know to do. I've tried giving Bill a dose of his own medicine. I met with an old boyfriend with the intention of using him to get revenge on Bill for cheating on me. But I felt so guilty, I couldn't "pull it off." I've screamed and yelled and refused to talk for days at a time, but nothing seems to work.

I cannot understand how another person can respond to the love that I give him with such dishonesty and disrespect. I feel *used* and *abused*. Bill says he loves me, but his behavior seems to say otherwise. I've tried to pray about this, but I am so angry that God allowed this to happen to me. I can't talk to my pastor because he would not understand, and I am so embarrassed.

The Life Lesson

Jesus said unto him, thou shalt love the Lord thy God with all thy heart, and with all thy soul, and with all thy mind. This is the first and great commandment (Matthew 22:37-38).

There is an old saying—I don't quite remember where it came from; I just know that it rings true—that goes: "The truth will set you free—but first, it will make you miserable." Often times, some of us allow ourselves to become involved in toxic relationships that are rooted more in addiction than affection. Behind our striving for success, recognition, relationship, and intimacy is the simple desire to be loved. We will do anything for it. Some of us will consult a psychic, get a new hairstyle, and read every "How to Get Him" book on the market. When love fails, we'll do anything to keep it, including cry, yell, and pout. Unfortunately, we seldom make a careful examination of why we continue to make the same mistakes over and over again. Before we run off to repeat another *love jones*, it is crucial that we examine our definition of love.

What is *love* anyway? How does it express itself in our lives? Does *love* arrive drunk on our doorsteps late at night? Does *love* drift in and out of our lives? Does *love* abuse us physically, emotionally, and spiritually? Does *love* hurt? Does *love* take without giving? Does *love* yearn for an unavailable mate?

A few years ago, a very popular and successful movie called *Fatal Attraction* depicted a woman who, after a short affair with a married man, developed such a fixation to him emotionally that her whole life became consumed with trying to possess him for herself. She went to such extremes as threatening him, trying to ruin his marriage, and even attempting to get him fired at work when he would not leave his wife and continue the affair. The consequence of a casual affair can be harmful and long-lasting. It is because of the awesome strength of the physical union between a man and a woman that God warns us in Proverbs:

...Wilt thou...embrace the bosom of a stranger? For the ways of a man are before the eye of the Lord...his own iniquities [sex sins] *shall take the wicked himself, and he shall be holden* [enslaved, tied] *with the cords of his sins* (Proverbs 5:20-22)

Realizing this, one can see why in Second Timothy 3:6 Paul says that women can be led captive by unscrupulous men (playboy hedonists): "For of this sort are they which creep into houses, and lead captive silly women [weak-natured and spiritually dwarfed women] laden with sins, led away with divers lusts." Lust and sin is gratifying for the moment, but a person always pays later in shame, guilt, humiliation, anger at self, anger at God, sorrow, and torment. It is often difficult for a person heavily involved in lust and self-gratification to see that she is only deceiving herself. Such a person often lives in a world of denial.

Sometimes people are unwilling to make a decision to change their life because they are actually addicted to lust. Years of sin have weakened their character to the point of destroying their desire for good. The harsh truth about love is that it is an emotion that cannot be forced. When a person does not want you, there is nothing that you can or cannot do to change that fact. However, the good news is that no matter how far into sin and lust a person has fallen, someone who has decided to serve the Lord with all her heart can be set free, with the help of the Lord.

First and foremost, one must understand that God is love and there can be no true understanding of love without a relationship with the One who is love. Love and lust are very different. Love is kind; lust is harsh. Love does not demand its own way; lust does. Our society confuses love and lust. Unlike lust, God's kind of love is directed outward toward others, not inward toward ourselves. It is utterly unselfish. In First Corinthians 13, Paul gives us the following list to describe what real love is like.

- Love suffereth long.
- Love envieth not.
- Love vaunteth not itself, is not puffed up.
- Love doth not behave itself unseemly.
- Love seeketh not its own.
- Love is not easily provoked.
- Love thinketh no evil.

- Love rejoiceth not in iniquity.
- Love beareth all things.
- Love hopeth all things.
- Love endureth all things.
- Love never fails.

This love is not natural. It is possible only if God supernaturally helps us set aside our own desires and instincts so we can give love while expecting nothing in return. Thus, the closer we come to Christ, the more love we will show to others. Any other type of love is a farce and a bogus imitation of the real thing. Don't try to "hold on" to things or people who want to go. Dysfunctional relationships are poison to the soul. Learn to release your anger in symbolic ways that are not destructive to you. Create a physical and psychic distance between yourself and that person.

- Tear up old photographs.
- Write his name on the bottom of your shoe and take a *long* walk.
- Start a love relationship with God.

Most of us have learned how to pretend to love others—how to speak kindly, avoid hurting others' feelings, and appear to take an interest in them. But God calls us to real love, which goes far beyond surface behaviors and emotions. Real love requires work and the investment of one's time. Healthy love demands our time, our money, and our personal involvement. And when you find yourself in a relationship with a person who does not give those things to you, you are not "in love" you are in "toxic love," which is deadly to the soul. There are a number of things you can do during those "dark nights of the soul" when you are tempted to "go back" for one more dose of toxic love:

- Call a friend and talk it out.
- Take a warm bath or take a long walk alone.
- Write in a journal.
- Exercise for 30 minutes.
- Talk to yourself. Tell yourself, "I can do better and I will."

In those weakest moments, when you begin to water down and sugar-coat all the bad times and overlook the insults and disrespect, pray this prayer:

Lord, help me to know the value of myself. Show me what real love is. Help me to first fall in love with You. Draw me closer to the One who loved me so much that He gave His life for me. In the lonely times, give me peace and comfort. Teach me how to delight myself in You, so that I can receive the desires of my heart according to Your will. Amen

A Tidbit of Wisdom

We only go after, and we only accept, what we think we deserve.

Story 14—Healing from Sexual Sin

The Story

*The Bible has a word for "safe sex": **marriage.***

Rosa's Story

I don't know what all the hoopla is about. I don't see anything wrong with engaging in sex outside of marriage. These are modern times. Sex is a beautiful expression of human intimacy that God gave us. If it were not meant to be enjoyed, God would not have created it for us. Every time I meet a nice young man, I admit that the first thing I think about is, *I wonder what he's like in bed.* On the first date I often find myself fantasizing about physical intimacy instead of listening to a guy's conversation.

I admit that this is probably not a good thing to do, but I really can't help myself. The men I date all expect to be sexually involved with me at some point. My choice is to hold on to archaic values like waiting to have sex after marriage or spend all my Saturday nights at home. I am a Christian, but I admit I have struggles in this area. I have been saved for about five years now, and I hope to find a good, Christian man and settle down soon in a marriage. I must admit I have been having a difficult time finding someone suitable. I just don't want to make the mistake of marrying someone who is sexually incompatible with me. I have girlfriends who say they are dissatisfied in their marriages because their husbands are sexually boring. I know what I'm doing is wrong in the sight of God, but I don't know what else to do. I believe in going after what I want. If I do nothing, I may end up old, childless, and alone.

I only get involved with men who go to church. And we keep our business private. I did have a steady boyfriend a year ago named Ron. We hit it off fine in the beginning. He is a member of my church. It was "love at first sight." He was everything I prayed for. We seemed so compatible. We spent the night together at his apartment after our third date. He was great. We even talked about moving in together and possibly getting married in the future. While we lived together we would keep our living arrangement a secret. After all, it's our personal business. No one around our church would have to know. Ron and I were great together—in the beginning. Then he began to change. I loved being with him sexually, but I did not like being with him as a friend.

Somewhere in the course of the relationship, I got bored. Ron seemed possessive and clingy. His constant nagging and insecurities were very aggravating. I just grew weary of a relationship that centered around sex and nothing else. We started to argue about little things. We lost respect for each other. Needless to say the relationship began to come apart at the seams, and Ron and I broke up before we seemed to get started. So, here I am again—looking.

The Life Lesson

Flee fornication. Every sin that a man doeth is without the body; but he that committeth fornication sinneth against his own body (1 Corinthians 6:18).

Sexual sin is no more sinful than any other sin, but its consequences may be more devastating. Sexual sin is not just between two consenting adults; it is an act of disobedience to God. Potiphar's wife failed to seduce Joseph into sexual sin. He resisted this temptation by saying, "It would be a great sin against God." Joseph did not say, "I'd be sinning against myself." When under pressure, those kinds of excuses are easily rationalized away.

There is none greater in this house than I; neither hath he kept back any-thing from me but thee, because thou art his wife; how then can I do this great wickedness, and sin against God? (Genesis 39:9)

Joseph avoided Potiphar's wife as much as possible. He refused her advances and finally ran from her. Sometimes merely trying to avoid temptation is not enough; we must turn and run, especially when the temptation may be too great for us. This is often the case in sexual temptations.

Sexual sins were dealt with swiftly and harshly in the Old Testament. God had no tolerance for such acts for the following reasons:

- They shatter the mutual commitment of married partners.
- They destroy the sanctity of the family.
- They twist people's mental well-being.
- They spread disease.

Sexual sin has always been widely available. Society's glorification of sex between people who are not married to each other often hides the fact that deep tragedy and hurt exist behind the scenes. When our culture portrays sexual sins as attractive, it is easy to forget what God said and why. The list of commands against sexual sins contained in Leviticus 20 includes extremely harsh punish-ments. Why? These detestable acts listed were very common in the heathen na-tions of Canaan; their religions were rampant with sex goddesses, temple prostitution, and other gross sins. God's answer and penalty for these sins was very clear and final as these examples show:

- Adultery (Lev. 20:10)—death.
- Incest (Lev. 20:11)—death.
- Homosexuality (Lev. 20:13)—death.
- Bestiality (Lev. 20:15)—death.

The Canaanite culture was destructive, and its people would not benefit the world. On the other hand, God was building a nation to make a positive influence on the world. So God prepared the people for what they would face in the Promised Land and commanded them against falling into the trap of such sexual sins. Anyone will agree that our society is inundated with sexually provocative material and messages. Sexual passion is a blessing from God to be acted upon in the context of marriage. However, sexual passion outside of marriage must be controlled. Don't allow sexual passion to boil over into evil actions.

What most of us call "love at first sight" is more clearly "lust at first sight." Human beings are designed by God to respond to sensory stimulation. We react to what we see, hear, taste, touch, and smell. True love, on the other hand, is rooted in friendship and companionship, not sensory stimulation alone.

In Genesis 34, Shechem the son of King Hamor the Hivite saw Dinah, one of Leah's daughters, as she visited some of her girlfriends. He watched her intently as she innocently cavorted with her friends. He allowed his sexual passion to boil over into evil actions. Shechem raped Dinah, and the consequences of his evil actions were far greater than he could have imagined. Dinah's brothers were outraged and took revenge. Pain, lying, deceit, and murder followed. Shechem may have been a victim of "love at first sight," but he acted on it with an impulsive, evil act. Not only did he sin against Dinah, he sinned against her entire family (see Gen. 34:6-7), which brought about severe consequences. Even Shechem's declared "love" for Dinah could not excuse the evil he did by forcibly raping her.

Paul recognized the importance of strong rules about sex for believers, because sexual sins have the power to bring disruption and destruction in the church.

Mortify therefore your members which are upon the earth; fornication, uncleanness, inordinate affection, evil concupiscence, and covetousness, which is idolatry. For which things' sake the wrath of God cometh on the children of disobedience (Colossians 3:5-6).

Sins involving sex are not innocent dabblings in forbidden pleasures, as so often portrayed, but they are powerful destroyers of relationships. They confuse and tear down the climate of respect, trust, and credibility that are so essential for solid marriages and secure children. In order to keep our natural, sexual passion under the control and subjection of Jesus Christ we must do the following:

1. Consider ourselves dead and unresponsive to evil desires.

2. Lay aside the old self and put on the new.

People should be able to see a difference between the way Christians and non-Christians live. Although we have a new nature, we don't automatically have all good thoughts and attitudes when we become new people in Christ.

Sex outside of marriage seems the "fashionable" thing to do. We are bombarded in the media with sexual images to such an extent that it seems like everyone is doing it. In some instances, the expectations about self-control seem to have changed over the years even in our churches. Sermons and workshops and classes about abstinence have been replaced with instruction about protection.

God has not changed His mind about sin due to public pressure. Fornication makes a mockery of God's original idea for sex. It treats sex as an isolated physical act rather than an act of commitment to another person. Outside of marriage, sex destroys relationships. Within marriage, it is a relationship builder. God frequently had to warn the people of Israel against the practice of fornication. Intimacy can create sexual feelings that overpower reason. Sometimes people are too often in a hurry to develop an intimate relationship based on their "strong feelings." But feelings are not enough to support a lasting relationship. We must patiently wait for feelings of love and commitment to develop together. Sexual intimacy outside of marriage causes the "feelings" of love and romance to grow faster than the commitment needed to make it last.

The Word of God is clear. Sex outside of marriage is sin. David asked God to search for sin and point it out even to the level of testing his thoughts. This is "exploratory surgery" for sin.

Search me, O God, and know my heart: try me, and know my thoughts: and see if there be any wicked way in me, and lead me in the way everlasting (Psalm 139:23-24).

How are we to recognize sin unless God points it out? Then when God shows us, we can repent and be forgiven. Make that scripture your prayer.

A Tidbit of Wisdom

Don't let what you do tonight make you sorry in the morning.

Story 15—The Joys of Stepparenting

The Story

A relationship is like a garden. It must be cultivated.

Cheryl's Story

Dave and I were married just six months ago, and already I'm ready to throw in the towel. I feel like we live in a zoo. I love Dave very much and he's a great guy, but this is not the marriage I bargained for. I knew Dave had three children, all teenagers from a previous marriage. They are good kids, or so I thought. And Dave seemed to get along well with my two children from my previous marriage. My children are young, only six and seven years old. Dave and I dated for two years. We wanted to make sure that marriage would work for us *this* time.

The communication between my husband and I is very good. We talk about everything. We discussed our living arrangement and the problems our "family blending" might bring so that we would ease the transition from a single-parent home to a two-parent family. It was only four months into our marriage that our world seemed to come crashing in on us. Dave's 16-year-old daughter is pregnant! Her mother threw her out of the house, and she showed up on our doorstep. Dave's three kids are good kids for the most part, but they are at that "crazy teenage stage" where they are testing and trying things to find their way in life. Dave's 15-year-old wants to stay out all hours of the night, and the 17-year-old is having trouble in school. Dave fears that he will not graduate. *I* think that he's experimenting with alcohol and marijuana, but Dave doesn't want to hear a lot of negative things about his teenage sons.

I find myself yelling at my own two children out of frustration. I've seen a definite change in their little personalities since all this occurred. All that aside, what am I going to do with two young children who don't understand what's going on? Dave's ex-wife is not cooperative. She's just glad her daughter is "out of her hair."

I feel trapped and cheated. My husband and I have prayed about this situation. He has agreed to do what I think is best. I feel sorry for the girl, but I also know that I have a home to maintain and a stable family to build too.

The Life Lesson

Except the Lord build the house, they labour in vain that build it... (Psalm 127:1).

The "Brady Bunch" was an idealized television family. It was not based on the real-life complexities and problems that occur when families are blended. Divorced people make up more than three out of every five single adults in America. That means the chances of dating and marrying someone who has been married before are very high, and with such a relationship will likely come ex-spouses and children. What's more, the types of marriages involving divorced men and women is almost limitless. Just for starters, there can be two divorced people, neither of whom have children, trying to make marriage work. There can also be one divorced person, without children, trying to form a relationship with someone who has never been married. Two divorced people, one with children and the other without them, or two divorced people, both with kids, could be trying to build a family together. Then, one must consider the tremendous variation in custody arrangements that exist today and the number of remarriages that result in still more children, making "family blending" extremely complex.

Statistics show that the divorce rate is highest among second marriages that involve blending families, and that divorce usually takes place within the first three years of marriage. Pretty scary! To survive in such a mixed-up environment, it is wise to follow a few basic rules:

1. Support your partner.
2. Act like a stepparent, if that's what you are.
3. Have a solid sense of your own level of comfort.
4. Accept at least the "possibility" that it may never work out the way you expected.

Support Your Partner

A husband and wife should always present themselves as a unit. They should always feel that they have the love and support of each other, even when there is a disagreement about how to handle situations within the family. Disagreements should be worked out behind closed doors. Support your partner, but don't take on problems that aren't really yours. If your partner's ex-spouse puts up one obstacle after another when one parent tries to spend time with the children, allow your spouse to work it out with his ex. He's her former spouse, not yours. Your husband will appreciate your understanding, support, and patience at these times. Let it be his problem to handle, and he will appreciate having a sympathetic ear in which to vent. Aim to show support and love, but don't try to fix somebody else's life unless you are invited to help problem-solve. Otherwise, it is a no-win situation. Be supportive, yet do not become directly involved.

Act Like a Stepparent, if That's What You Are

You may ultimately become a good buddy, or even a trusted friend to your partner's children. But you will never be their other parent, and don't try to be. It can take up to two years to earn your stepchildren's trust and respect. Granted, there are not many positive images out there on which to model yourself. From our earliest childhood, we all memorize fairy-tale legends of wicked stepmothers and cruel stepfathers. But those stories don't have to set the limits of the relationship you will have with one another. With lots of effort and creativity, you can define what works best for all of you. Remember, though, it is your mate who fell in love with you. The children did not. Don't expect them to. However, it is reasonable to expect them to act responsibly and to show respect toward your mate.

Have a Solid Sense of Your Own Level of Comfort

Have a solid sense of your acceptable "can-do's" and intolerable "can't do's." The time will come when you and your spouse will need to set standards and develop a long-range strategy to handle discipline, especially if both of you were single parents. It is likely that you may have different expectations and styles of discipline. A common mistake new mates make is in the area of discipline. Children, under the best of conditions, do not like to be corrected. It is up to you and your spouse to determine in advance and away from the children how you are going to handle these kinds of issues. It is absolutely essential that the children view you both as a team that cannot be divided and conquered. Engage in many conversations before marriage about the responsibilities and expectations of being in a relationship with someone with children.

Accept at Least the Possibility That It May Never Work Out

Sometimes we want so much for the connection to be right that we refuse to admit defeat. Like it or not, you may need to realize that the best you can hope for is that your new spouse's children will only tolerate you. When all the effort that you have invested in the partnership falls short, causes you more harm than good, and more negative energy is being expended than positive, then it is time to do some serious evaluation. Perhaps the children won't ever accept or like you. If that is true, then go back to the first rule: Don't take on problems that are not yours. It is their problem and not yours. Just as you must take responsibility for choosing to love somebody who has been married and/or has children, your partner must assume responsibility for loving you—whether children like you or not. If your spouse cannot assume that responsibility, then the real problem has to do with the mate, not his children.

Maintaining contact with a former spouse because of the children can be very uncomfortable. Divorce can be a death that is never complete. It tends to recur with each family contact, after which the relationship dies all over again. However, for the sake of the family and the emotional health of the children involved, the lines of communication *must* remain open. It is essential to maintain a cooperative relationship with the ex-spouse. Some of these guidelines can help:

- Work out the specifics of custody, visitation, and living arrangements before the divorce (mediation services or mental health professionals are often more helpful in this regard than lawyers).
- Cooperate on the visitation schedule and on discipline.
- Don't criticize the other parent in front of the children.
- Communicate often and honestly with your children.
- Explain to the children that you have not divorced them.
- Reassure children that the divorce was not their fault.
- Recognize that a new family arrangement is upsetting to grown children too.
- Make prayer a precedent in your new family.

One of the greatest resources God has given us is the family. The family provides acceptance, encouragement, exhortation, and counsel. If our faith in Christ is real, it will usually prove itself at home, in our relationships with those who know us best. Children and parents have a responsibility to each other.

Children, obey your parents in the Lord: for this is right. Honor thy father and mother: which is the first commandment with promise (Ephesians 6:1-2).

Children should honor their parents, even if the parents are demanding and unfair. Parents should care gently for their children, even if the children are disobedient and unpleasant. Ideally, Christian parents and children will relate to each other with thoughtfulness and love. There is a difference between *obeying* and *honoring*. To *obey* means to do as one is told. To *honor* means to show respect and love. Children are to obey until they are no longer under their parents' care, but the responsibility to honor parents continues for a lifetime.

The purpose of parental discipline is to help children grow, not to hurt or discourage them. Parenting is not easy, and parenting in a new, blended family is even more difficult. It takes a lot of patience to raise children in a loving Christ-honoring manner. But frustration and anger should not be causes for discipline. Instead, parents should act in love, treating their children as Jesus treats the people that He loves. This is vital to children's development and to their concept of the Lord. If children are brought up in the nurture and admonition of the Lord and the home is build upon a love for God and the principles of His Word, even a blended family is a source of acceptance, encouragement, exhortation, and counsel. For those who are facing the struggles of a blended family, pray this prayer:

Lord, bless this family and the relationship that we have with each other. Guide us as parents to nourish our children with wholesome discipline and instruction that will bend them toward God and Christian living. Help us to build our family upon the solid foundation of Jesus Christ. Help us to seek cooperation, act in love, and react with kindness. Amen.

A Tidbit of Wisdom

Children don't divide a couple's love—they multiply it.

Story 16—Waiting for a Good Man

The Story

Don't kiss a fool, and never let a fool kiss you.

Deborah's Story

I've had my share of "bad men." I admit that I sowed some pretty wild oats in my day. The most compelling question of my adolescence was, "Is he cute?" The fact is, on the "he's gotta have it" list nothing else came close to looks. Having a man who was attractive was my priority. Consequently, I ended up in a lot of bad relationships with men who were irresponsible, weak, lazy, self-centered, and who ran at the first mention of commitment. My mother always said, "A weak man is like a pair of cheap panty hose; at the first sign of stress, they run." And she was right. But that was then and this is now.

I celebrated my thirty-ninth birthday last week. I am amazed at how quickly it came. I thought surely I skipped a few years. Time seemed to speed up after 35, and I found myself still single and looking. There is an old adage that says: "Men love the women they are attracted to; women are attracted to the men they love." Today at 39, "cute" is way down at the bottom of my "he's gotta have it" list. Now I look for someone who is honest, hard-working, has good character, integrity, and is capable of commitment. A man's physical attractiveness is not important to me at all.

I have my head together. I know what I want and what I need. A woman's idea of what makes a man desirable changes with age. I know what a good man is now. A good man has the following qualities:

- He is there for the long haul, not just the moment.
- He is self-assured without being self-absorbed.
- He can keep a promise, a secret, and a job.
- He can bring home the bacon *and* fry it up in the pan.
- He is passionate about his work and his woman and never neglects one for the other.
- He treats women as equals.
- He can tell the difference between a rhinestone and a diamond—in jewelry and people.
- He will compromise his viewpoint but not his values.
- He takes care of his children by choice, not force.

So where are all the good men! I feel so anxious and nervous about this issue that I have seriously considered just taking the best man I can find. If he has at least six or seven good qualities out of ten, that is better than having no man at all. This waiting game seems to be getting the best of me. I've even thought about calling a few old boyfriends and maybe taking a second look at one of them. At least I would feel like I'm making some progress.

I must admit, I never thought that I would find myself in this predicament. Maybe God does not want me to be happy. I've prayed about it, but God does not seem to be listening. I feel like giving up.

The Life Lesson

Wait on the Lord: be of good courage, and He shall strengthen thine heart: wait, I say on the Lord (Psalm 27:14).

At one time or another, every one of us has had to wait on something, whether we did so patiently or in a state of aggravated anxiety. We have waited for healing, husbands, salvation of loved ones, improvement of finances—we've all had to wait on God for something.

There probably isn't anything harder to do than to wait, whether we are expecting something good, or an unknown. One way we often cope with a long wait (or even a short one) is to begin to help God get His plan into action. Sarah tried this approach (see Gen. 16). She was too old to expect to have a child of her own, so she thought God must have something else in mind. From Sarah's limited point of view, this could only be to give Abraham a son through another woman—a common practice in her day. The plan seemed harmless enough. Abraham would sleep with Sarah's slave girl (Hagar), who would then give birth to a child. Sarah would take the child as her own. The plan worked beautifully, at first, but Sarah lived to regret trying to push God's timetable ahead.

Another way we cope with a long wait is to gradually conclude that what we are waiting for is never going to happen. Sarah waited 90 years for a baby. When God told her that she would finally have one of her own, she laughed—not so much from a lack of faith in what God could do, but from doubt about what He could do through her.

Therefore Sarah laughed within herself, saying, After I am waxed old shall I have pleasure, my lord being old also? (Genesis 18:12)

When confronted about her laughter, Sarah lied—as she had seen her husband do from time to time. She probably did not want her true feelings to be known. What part of your life seems to be on hold right now? Do you understand that this may be God's plan for you? The Bible has more than enough clear direction to keep us busy while waiting for some particular part of our life to move ahead.

People often wonder if it is worth it to wait a long time for something they truly desire. Jacob waited seven years to marry Rachel. After being tricked, he agreed to work seven more years for her. For Jacob, the blessing of Rachel as his wife was worth the wait.

And Jacob served seven years for Rachel; and they seemed unto him but a few days, for the love he had to her (Genesis 29:20).

The most important goals and desires are worth waiting and paying for. Movies and television have created the illusion that people have to wait only an hour or two to solve their problems or to get what they want. Don't be trapped into thinking the same is true in real life. Patience is hardest when we need it most, but it is the key to achieving goals.

David knew from experience what it meant to wait on the Lord. He had been anointed king at age 16, but he did not become king until he was 30. During the interim, he was chased through the wilderness by jealous King Saul (see 1 Sam. 23:14). Later, after becoming king, he was chased by his rebellious son Absalom. (see 2 Sam. 15:14) David had to wait on God for the fulfillment of the promise that he would reign. Waiting on God is not easy. Often it seems that God is not answering our prayers or does not understand the urgency of our situation. That kind of thinking implies that God is not in control or is not fair. But God is worth waiting for. The prophet Isaiah tells us to, because often God uses waiting to refresh, renew, and teach us.

But they that wait upon the Lord shall renew their strength... (Isaiah 40:31).

Make good use of your waiting times by discovering what God may be trying to teach you in them. David received these four benefits from waiting on God (see Ps. 40:1-4):

1. God lifted him out of his despair.
2. God set his feet on firm ground.
3. God steadied his walk.
4. God gave him a new purpose.

Often these blessings cannot be received unless we go through the trial of waiting. While we are waiting for answers to prayer or for difficult situations to change, we can *pray for patience and insight* and *seek God's guidance*.

Waiting for God to work does not mean sitting around doing nothing. We must do what we can while we can as long as we do not run ahead of God. God may seem slow to us as we face situations that seem to need God's immediate answers and attention. But God is not slow; He just is not on our timetable.

A Tidbit of Wisdom

Everything comes to him who hustles while he waits. Don't settle for half of a person and try to make him whole. Don't go to the altar hoping to alter your mate.

Story 17—Getting off the Love Merry-Go-Round

The Story

Everything good to you ain't good for you.
When someone leaves, God's making room for something better.

Frederica's Story

He was like no one I had ever met. The world stopped when I first saw him across a crowded room at an art exhibit. We stared at each other. Our eyes consumed each other's soul. I was driven to make him mine for all eternity. I planned each day to give him the last ounce of my spirit. I knew that we were destined to be together. He was my life. If he called, I dropped everything and ran. I adopted his beliefs and principles. He would creep into every conversation with my friends. I was fulfilled when I made sacrifices for him. He only gave a little bit, but that was enough for me.

Then one day he found someone else. I thought my life would never be the same again. I turned my back on the world and retreated into my shell. I swore that I would never love again...a month later...he was like no one I had ever met. The world stopped when I first saw him across a crowded room—here we go again.

I realize, among other things, that I have a tendency to attract men who are like little lost puppies. There was a time in my life when men would come into my life and expect me to support them financially. I had to take responsibility for allowing this behavior. I realize that I like to fix needy and out-of work men and nurse them back to health. I know I need to close the Frederica Jones Savings and Loan Association because of too many withdrawals in the loan department and zero return on my investments.

The Life Lesson

The eyes of the Lord are upon the righteous, and His ears are open unto their cry (Psalm 34:15).

Negative patterns in our relationships may be familiar, but they do not represent love. Only when we learn to have a loving relationship with ourselves can we expect to attract love from others. Most of us have had our fill of destructive relationships. We can choose to be bitter, or we can agree that life is a series of choices, and choose not to be. Each of us must examine the attitudes and behaviors that contribute to our allowing unhealthy relationships in our life.

Let's face it, no one said that relationships are easy. We are all making our way, trying to find joy. When we encounter stumbling blocks, instead of blaming each other, we should examine ourselves. If we offer ourselves as fractured and less than whole, then we attract to ourselves a mirror of what we are. If you don't enjoy your own company, nobody else will. If you don't value yourself, nobody else will. Many of us make the mistake of spending an inordinate amount of time polishing our external selves. If we learn to "begin at the beginning" by understanding that we are God's creation and that He made us with great care and purpose, we will begin to place a greater value on ourselves as the objects of God's love. David valued himself as a human being because he realized how precious he was to God:

I will praise thee; for I am fearfully and wonderfully made...my substance was not hid from Thee, when I was made in secret, and curiously wrought in the lowest parts of the earth. ... How precious also are Thy thoughts unto me, O God! How great is the sum of them! (Psalm 139:14-15,17)

David thanked God for making him so wonderfully complex. It is amazing to think about how God was there when we were being formed in utter seclusion in our mother's womb. God saw us before we were born and scheduled every day of our life before we began to breathe. How precious it is to realize that God is constantly thinking about every individual. We should have as much respect for ourselves as our Maker has for us. When someone you love is thinking about you all the time, it comforts you. If God thinks about us this much, shouldn't we find time to think about Him each day?

Only when we examine how we feel about ourselves will we be able to stop making the same mistakes in our relationships. How we feel about ourselves determines the quality of our present and future relationships. People in our lives perceive our self-perception and treat us accordingly. Although we desire happy relationships, if we continue with the same patterns of behavior, we will, without realizing it, create cycles of despair.

As we begin to truly value our lives, we will only surround ourselves with those who treat us well. Breaking old habits by getting off the "love merry-go-round" is not easy, but when they are bad, old habits, breaking them can be more than worthwhile. God's character goes into the creation of every person. When you feel worthless or even begin to hate yourself, remember that God's Spirit is ready and willing to work within you to make your character all that God meant it to be. Begin to have a loving relationship with yourself. Take time to nurture and pamper you.

- Buy yourself a bouquet of flowers.
- Take time to take *you* on a date.
- Take time out to listen to you…to hear your own breath.
- Talk to God like a good friend every day.
- Get a massage.
- Pamper yourself.

A Tidbit of Wisdom

You attract what you are—fix yourself.

Story 18—Surviving Spousal Abuse

The Story

There are those who look into the abyss and choose to live.

Sharon's Story

Divorce! The very sound of the word sounds like profanity. I never dreamed that such a tragedy would happen to my life because I am a pastor's wife. I did everything right. I prayed and asked God to guide me in my choice of a husband. I waited patiently. I did not enter into my decision to marry unadvisedly. I asked all the right questions. I did everything right, and yet, I find myself a part of the most frightening statistic of modern times—the high divorce rate and the subsequent dissolution of the family.

My husband is involved in a homosexual relationship with another man. Somewhere in the back of my mind, I knew something about our relationship as a man and woman was just not right. I could never put my finger on it, but something always seemed strange. Homosexuality was the last thing on my mind.

I found hotel receipts and strange letters in his briefcase. Still, I would not allow myself to even consider such a horrible thing. My world was shattered when I came home early from a visit with my parents and caught my husband and his lover embracing in our bedroom. I left in a rage, angry and embarrassed at what I had seen.

I confronted my husband the next day. He pushed me to the floor and threatened me if I told anyone. That's when the violence started. I know that when a man hits a woman once, he will continue to use violence as a means of control. After a black eye and a busted lip, I decided to leave.

I feel like such a failure. If only I could run away and start over with a new life somewhere, then no one would know how badly I messed up my old one. All I want to do is make him pay for what he's done to me emotionally. I feel so cheated and angry. I feel totally worthless and rejected. If only I could find some explanation or point to some reason why this has happened to me, I think I could live with it better. When I felt the relationship turning sour, I did all the correct things. I prayed, I fasted, I interceded. I anointed his pillow. I evaluated my own behavior. I bought new lingerie and got a new hairstyle. I made sure dinner was always on the table on time. I did everything I knew to do, and divorce still came crashing into my life like a boulder rushing down a mountainside. I feel like my life has been stolen from me. I've heard of other pastor's wives suffering from an abusive husband, but I never thought I would be one. I have no one to talk to about my situation.

I can't help but feel angry at myself for not intuitively knowing that Richard was wrong for me. I beat myself up constantly for misreading the signs or maybe seeing the signs and not acknowledging them. I was always the one who championed the institution of marriage. I sang its praises to anyone who would listen and condemned those who, for whatever reason, couldn't "hang in there" and make it work. I bragged about what a good husband I had and how happy I was. My commitment to him and our marriage was total and unwavering. I assumed that he felt the same way and had the same values—he said he did. I've only been divorced for eight months now, and yet the guilt, humiliation, and loneliness are overwhelming. I don't know whether or not to change my last name back to my maiden name because my ex-husband is well known. Should I stop wearing my wedding ring? I don't know how "not to be a couple.'' What about our friends? Do we divide them up like the furniture in the living room? Divorce feels like death, only worse. I am now living in a city where I don't know anyone. I've spent several months trying to find a church where no one knows my ex-husband. I feel so vulnerable and alone. I have no hope of ever being happy again.

The Life Lesson

...God hath called us to peace (1 Corinthians 7:15b).

When people marry, they expect their bond to last forever. Ripping the bond apart through divorce is a devastating, wrenching experience. Divorce is one of the most stressful situations a person can undergo. Yet we can go through divorce or grow through divorce. If you apply all your strength to the task of redefining your life, you will gain a sense of self and discover a resilience that you never knew you had. You will also be able to begin healing the painful wounds of divorce.

Divorce is as harmful and destructive today as it was in Jesus' day. God intends marriage to be a lifetime commitment.

Therefore shall a man leave his father and his mother, and shall cleave unto his wife and they shall be one flesh (Genesis 2:24).

In Moses' day, as well as in Jesus' day, the practice of marriage fell short of God's intention. The same is true today. Staying together in marriage was God's intention, but because human nature made divorce inevitable, Moses instituted some laws to help its victims.

When a man hath taken a wife, and married her, and it come to pass that she find no favour in his eyes...then let him write her a bill of divorcement, and give it in her hand, and send her out of his house. And when she is departed...she may go and be another man's wife (Deuteronomy 24: 1-2).

These were civil laws designed especially to protect the women who, in that culture, were quite vulnerable when living alone. With Moses' law, a man could no longer just throw his wife out—he had to write a formal letter of dismissal.

God allowed divorce as a concession to people's sinfulness. Divorce was instituted to protect the injured party in the midst of a bad situation. God wants married people to consider their marriage permanent. However, not all spouses honor God's Word or live by God's laws. It is not God's intention that we remain lifelong victims in marital situations plagued with abuse. Paul encourages the Christian spouse to try to get along with the unbelieving spouse and make the marriage work. If, however, the unbelieving spouse insists on leaving the marriage physically and/or emotionally, Paul says to let him or her go.

But if the unbelieving depart, let him depart. A brother or a sister is not under bondage in such cases: but God hath called us to peace (1 Corinthians 7:15).

The only alternative would be for the Christian to deny her faith to preserve her marriage, and this would be the one thing worse than dissolving the marriage.

Once you realize that "divorce is really happening to me and is not just some statistic," you will most likely feel shock. Some people prolong this stage by clinging to false hopes that they and their spouse will get back together again, that things will work out, and that there will be a happy ending. Try to look realistically at your situation as it is, not as you want it to be. Honesty is essential.

Understand that God does not "throw anyone away" no matter what you've done or what you've experienced. God understands that we as believers live in a fallen world and sometimes the sins and disobedience of others damage our lives as well. We are not insulated from the world or its evil affects. Divorce is ugly. The journey through it is excruciating. When people have worked through it, they will bear scars. But they will also feel cleansed, unburdened, and full of hope. As strange as it may seem, people who travel this jagged road are almost always enriched. They are more realistic, more compassionate, more profoundly human. Amid the upheaval and the chaos, God is present. Out of weakness, we can find strength, and out of our confusion, we can find a purpose.

The church can present another obstacle for divorced persons. You might feel so condemned by the laws of your church that you feel alienated from other believers, just at a time when you need them the most. A compassionate minister from your church might be able to help restore your faith in a loving God who is always there to sustain you.

Learn to redefine your life. No matter how desperate, guilty, or lonely you may feel now, if you accept the challenge of beginning anew, you are sure to come to a deeper understanding of yourself. You will see that you are a viable, strong, and sound person. You will learn to love yourself again. Divorce is not an *event* in a courtroom, but a process of recovery. And you must walk through the *process* one minute, one hour, one day at a time.

- Funeralize the relationship.
- Take all the time you need to grieve.
- Adjust to new patterns of living.
- Create a support system.
- Turn to God.

Funeralize the Relationship

Verbally acknowledge the death of your marriage to yourself. When left unburied, dead things smell bad and pollute the environment. Admit to yourself that you are divorced and take responsibility for your life as it is now. As in a regular funeral, remember the good things about your spouse, then close the emotional casket and perform the last rites. To exhume that emotional corpse is like calling up dead things.

Take All The Time You Need To Grieve

Take time to grieve. There is a mourning period in divorce that is very similar to mourning the loss of a mate through death. Regardless of the circumstances of your divorce—who instigated it, how inevitable it was, etc., you have lost something important, and you need to grieve. Denying or suppressing your feelings of sorrow will only extend this phase of your recovery. Beware of "negative mourning," which is wallowing in self-pity or blame, where everything was either your fault or someone else's. This can prolong the grief period and lead to deep depression.

Adjust To New Patterns of Living

Acknowledge the practical concerns of life after divorce like moving, living at a reduced income, making child care arrangements, taking on additional household responsibilities, and finding new employment. Give yourself the time you need to make the appropriate adjustments for you. Work out a strategy and a game plan to tackle each problem and new life situation presented as a result of your divorce. Then get busy.

Create a Support System

Because your divorce affects the whole network of people that you and your spouse knew, you may find yourself suddenly cut off from some friends and relatives. Make new friends! Associate with happy, healthy people. Join a new church, start a hobby, go places with groups, show yourself friendly. Feel free to seek professional counseling. There is great comfort in learning from a professional that other people have gone through what you are now going through and survived. A good counselor can give you valuable insights into yourself and your situation. As helpful as friends and counselors can be, they cannot go through your divorce for you, however. It is essentially a "do it yourself" process.

Turn To God

Going through a divorce provides a tremendous opportunity to reach out to God. He is your greatest source of inner strength and loves you infinitely more than you have ever loved anyone. Turn to God often, not lingering on questions like "Why did this happen to me?" but with questions like "How can I make this situation better?" and "What can I learn from this?" Turn to God to help you deal with the bitterness that you might feel toward your former spouse. The "revenge factor" can often derail the recovery process. The divorce can become a never-ending battle that inhibits personal growth and harms other people involved. Even though *you* may be incapable of forgiving your former spouse, God can accomplish this in you if you set your heart in that direction. Pray this prayer for strength when experiencing divorce:

Lord, I ask for peace and comfort during this difficult time. I know that You love me and understand the pain that I am feeling. Thank You for forgiveness and mercy. Remove any bitterness that I may have for those who have offended me. Heal me emotionally. Help me to love and trust again. Amen.

A Tidbit of Wisdom

Life breaks us all sometimes, but some grow strong at broken places.

Chapter 5

The Leftovers

For this is the word of promise... (Romans 9:9)

Any good cook knows that everything that is edible is useful if she is creative enough to look beyond what seems useless to see the potential in the scraps and the leftovers.

I remember my grandmother making sweet pickles from the rind of watermelons. She would actually take the watermelon rinds thrown away after the evening meal, wash, peel, and cut them up into bite-sized cubes. Then she would add secret ingredients from the herbs and spices of her garden. She would place this concoction in jars filled with spring water and seal the lids tightly. These jars sat in the shed behind her house, lined up on weather-beaten shelves, sometimes for years. The longer they sat, the sweeter and tastier the rinds became. Every time I saw my grandmother's watermelon rind pickles, I would appreciate her ability to look at something someone else would regard as "useless" and make something "useful" out of it.

My grandmother used that same insight and creativity with the leftover drippings of the meat she cooked for those special Sunday dinners. When the meat was well-cooked and golden brown, she would drain off the juice at the bottom of the pan and set it aside in a jar. She called it the "pan drippings." It looked dirty and useless because it was greasy and full of fragments and debris from the cooked meat. But grandma always knew what to do with the "leftovers." "Everything is useful for something," she would say. Then with a little flour, some water, and a few family secrets, she would turn the pan drippings into the finest tasting gravy, which added the needed flavor to bring out the best in the meat. Long after the meat was gone, everyone around the dinner table could be seen scraping their bread across the plate to get the last drop of gravy.

Sometimes painful events in our lives are experiences that we just want to forget. We want to put the betrayals, the disappointments, the failures, and the bad choices out with the garbage to be hauled away and never to be seen or thought of again. However, a wise person knows that no experience in life is useless. When you are in the midst of a painful experience, all you feel is the hurt, anger, and confusion of what you are going through. It seems ludicrous to expect anything good to come out of the situation. We want to put the tears, sleepless nights, and emotional torment behind us. But the passage of time gives us an opportunity to distance ourselves from the mental and emotional anguish. It has been said that time heals all wounds—and it does. The passage of time seems to dull the pain of situations that seemed unbearable at the time.

Looking at a painful experience in a new and creative way can provide a valuable *life lesson* to pass on to someone else. When we look back, we give ourselves an opportunity to look at a painful situation and finally say, "Now, Lord, I understand why You allowed that to happen in my life." Usually it is only after we are out of a difficult situation where we felt alone and abandoned do we realize that God was with us all along. What matters is not so much the events or circumstance of life, but our response to them.

With God's help, any situation, no matter how heartbreaking, can be used for good—even when others intend it for evil. Joseph's story in Genesis is an excellent example of this principle. As a youngster, Joseph was overconfident. His natural self-assurance, which was increased by being Jacob's favorite son and by knowing of God's plan for his life, was unbearable to his ten older brothers, who eventually conspired against him. They were angry over the possibility of being ruled by their little brother. Finding Joseph in a field one day, they seized him and sold him to slave traffickers from Egypt.

Joseph could not understand how his brothers could do such a thing to their own flesh and blood. When he heard them bickering over the price, he begged them not to go through with it, but they would not listen. They handed him over to the slave traffickers, counted the money, and divided it among themselves as Joseph was handcuffed and taken away.

Joseph was 17 years old when he was sold into slavery by his brothers. He spent 11 years as an Egyptian slave and 2 years in prison. He became governor of Egypt when he was 30. Joseph rose quickly to the top—from prison walls to Pha-raoh's palace. His training for this important position involved being first a slave and then a prisoner. But his self-assurance, molded by pain and combined with a personal knowledge of God, allowed him to survive and prosper where most would have failed. Perhaps you can identify with one or more of these hardships Joseph experienced: He was betrayed and deserted by loved ones, exposed to sexual temptation, and punished for doing the right thing. He endured a long imprisonment and was forgotten by those he had helped. Joseph's positive response transformed each setback into a step forward. He did not spend much time asking "Why?" His approach was, "What shall I do now?" When you are facing a setback, the beginning of a Joseph-like attitude is to acknowledge that God is with you. There is nothing like God's presence to shed new light on a dark situation.

After many years of hardship, Joseph learned an important lesson: Because our talents and knowledge come from God, it is more appropriate to thank Him for them than to brag about them. As a young boy, Joseph was boastful about his dreams. As a man, he no longer flaunted his superior status. Although Joseph's brothers wanted to get rid of him, God used even their evil actions to fulfill His ultimate plan. He sent Joseph ahead to preserve their lives, save Egypt, and prepare the way for the beginning of the nation of Israel. God is sovereign. His plans are not dictated by human actions. When others intend evil toward you, remember, they are only God's tools. Joseph finally said to his brothers,

> *But as for you, ye thought evil against me; but God meant it unto good, to bring to pass, as it is this day, to save much people alive* (Genesis 50:20).

Whatever your situation, no matter how undesirable, consider it part of your training program for serving God. Every experience is useful for serving God. Ask God to show you how you can better serve Him by looking at painful experiences in new and creative ways. God will give you a "look back" in due time. Pray this prayer for encouragement:

> *Dear Lord, I acknowledge that You are always with me. When I do not understand painful situations in my life, help me to remember that You are sovereign and therefore working this out for my good. Thank You for on-the-job training to serve You. Amen.*

CRowTh CRound

I have found trouble to be growth ground. *Growth ground* means a foundation, or place, to grow. Pain and hardship are like soil where good character, strength, and endurance are planted and grow. Trouble can be a foundation or "ground" where something positive can develop. When trouble comes, we are forced to learn, forced to resolve, forced to derive some order out of the chaos. Pain is an experience that is never wasted. Often times, it is not until we put some distance of time between the experience and the lesson that we learn from it can we see the significance and necessity for it and the hand of the Lord in it. Paul encourages us in Romans:

> *And we know that all things work together for good to them that love God, to them who are the called according to **His** purpose* (Romans 8:28).

This does not mean that all that happens to us is good. Evil is prevalent in our fallen world, but God is able to turn every negative situation around for *our long-range good*. Note that God is not working to make us happy, but to fulfill His purpose. Note also that His promise is not for everybody. It can be claimed only by those who love God and who are fitting into God's plans. Such people have a new perspective, a new mind-set on life. They trust in God, not life's treasures; they look to their security in Heaven not on earth; they learn to accept pain and persecution on earth, not resent it, because it brings them closer to God. God works all things out—not just isolated incidents—for our good.

God's ultimate goal for us is to make us like Christ. As we become more and more like Him, we discover our true selves, the persons we were created to be. If one wants to be successful in life, one must learn from those who have achieved success. For example, if you want to learn how to play the piano, you would not go to ten people who failed and ask, "May I study your failures, so I can learn to be successful?" You would go to those who have mastered the instrument, seeking to learn their techniques.

One challenge that the believer faces is similar to that experienced by the 12 tribes of Israel who wandered for 40 years because they lost faith. When they sent out scouts to the Promised Land, all but two, Joshua and Caleb, returned fearful of what they believed existed. They saw large fruit. They cut down a single cluster of grapes so large that it took two of them to carry it on a pole between them. They saw giants. The land was occupied by the Ahimanites, Sheshites, and Talmites, all families descended from Anak the giant. They discouraged the people from continuing.

But the men that went up with him said, We be not able to go up against the people; for they are stronger than we (Numbers 13:31).

Only two of the scouts saw the promise that the land held and saw it as God's fulfillment of His covenant with Israel. Their views were unpopular with the people. However, they were the only two adults of their generation who entered the Promised Land with the children of the others. The rest of their generation perished. There are at least two lessons that we can learn from this:

1. We are similarly lost if we focus only on our failures and do not allow ourselves to see the vision of what is possible.
2. We must learn to appreciate difficulties and challenges in our lives.

Difficulties and challenges shape us into what and who we are to be if we learn that they are not coincidences but are somehow part of God's sovereign plan to form Christ in us. Thus problems are not merely situations that we "go through," but rather they are opportunities for us to "grow through." Problems in life are God's tools to help us understand that we are really sharing with Christ. Joseph chose to grow through his problems. It would have been easy for him to be filled with hatred toward his brothers. Thankfully, he concluded that it was better to forgive than to hate. The betrayal Joseph felt when his brothers bartered his liberties away was enormous. Rather than holding a grudge and hoping for a day of revenge, he chose to forgive. What a blessed choice that turned out to be. Forgiveness drew the poison out, removing all desire for revenge. Forgiveness is a wonderful thing. It allows healing to flow and wholeness to return at the deepest levels of the relationship. When you forgive, you set the prisoner free. And, strangely enough, the prisoner you end up freeing most is yourself.

Handling Hurt

A number of options are open to us when it comes to handling hurt in our lives. We can handle hurt in one of these three ways:

- internalize
- retaliate
- forgive

Internalize

The first thing that we can do with our hurts is *internalize* them. We can grit our teeth, hold up our chin, and repress the pain that we feel, pretending all is well when it isn't. When hurt is internalized or placed in a reserve of unresolved anger, it causes resentment, bitterness, and hostility to take root in our lives. Like toxic waste, it poisons from within, inch by inch. Like a boiler whose valve has been turned off, it generates an enormous amount of internal pressure that may explode when exposed to only a minor provocation. The hurts that we receive can have either a positive or a negative effect; they can make us *bitter*, or they can make us *better*. I have often heard it said that if you internalize the hurt and pain of your youth, one day you will meet up with a bitter, old, cantankerous person—and it will be you. When I think of what hurt can do to an individual when it is internalized, my best friend from grade school comes to mind.

Sharon was my dear friend when we were in elementary school. I knew her to be a sweet little girl in fifth grade, quick to smile and fun to play with. She was simply delightful to be around. After meeting her some 25 years later, I knew that life had been unkind to her. She had become the "community crazy lady." She had a sour personality and was full of cynicism, suspicion, and mistrust. We talked briefly. The world, as she saw it, was out to get her. Holding a conversation with her was difficult. I could not believe this was the same person. She asked the rhetorical question, "How are you?" with a scowl on her face, which let me know that she was not really interested in how I was doing. I answered with the customary, "Fine, thank you" and began enumerating upon the wonderful blessings of the past 25 years—only to have her to break in with a laundry list of "who did what to her and when." Over the years, sweet little Sharon had turned into a cynical old buzzard who was angry with the world.

Have you ever met anyone who is so down on life that they are painful to be around? How did they get this way? They were not born like that. The hurts they received over the years were internalized. When we fail to cope with hurt in our lives, it has a corrosive effect upon our personality. The negative spirit and attitude that results is nothing more than an outward reflection of the bottled-up resentment that we hold inside.

We are all familiar with the story of Job and his wife. The Lord gave satan permission to test Job in a particularly harsh manner.

And the Lord said unto Satan, Behold, all that he hath is in thy power; only upon himself put not forth thine hand. So Satan went forth from the presence of the Lord (Job 1:12).

God allowed Job and his wife to experience the deepest kind of hurt. The things they worked for all their lives—their servants, their cattle, their camels— were all taken away by invaders in one day. Then came the terrible news that their ten children had been killed in a violent storm. Their whole world came crashing in around them. There is no way to fathom the grief that they felt. Ten children were lined up in ten different caskets all on the same day. The depth of their pain boggles my mind. When the funeral was over, the brokenhearted couple returned home Mrs. Job said to her husband, "You can go on serving God if you wish, but you can count me out." As she saw it, God had let her down. She felt they deserved better from Him than they had received. As far as she was concerned, God was no longer worthy of their devotion. Job tried to convince her otherwise. He tried to persuade her that God must have had a reason for allowing what had happened.

Instead of casting herself upon God's goodness and mercy and saying, "I don't understand why You have allowed this to happen, but I'm going to trust You in the midst of it," Job's wife became angry. "We served God faithfully all these years," she told her husband, "and this is what we get. No thanks. When it comes to serving God, from now on you can do it alone."

Then said [Job's] *wife unto him, Dost thou still retain thine integrity? curse God, and die* (Job 2:9).

About the time Job's emotional wounds were beginning to heal he came down with boils. From the crown of his head to the soles of his feet, he was covered with painful boils. Seeing her husband suffer like this was more than Job's wife could bear. She was furious with God for allowing this to happen, and she wanted Job to curse God to his face and lie down and die so he could find relief from his terrible pain. The hurts she had received embittered her spirit and she internalized her pain. Yet Job knew that God somehow was making a better man out of him in his furnace of affliction. Job was so confident of God's goodness that he said:

Though He slay me, yet will I trust in Him (Job 13:15).

Finally, after hours of praying and sobbing, Job came to the place in his heart where he could look up to Heaven and say, "Not my will, but thy will be done. My heart is broken, but I haven't lost faith in Your wisdom, in Your goodness, or in Your power. You are the Creator; I am the creature. You are the Potter; I am the clay. Your will is supreme. From the depths of my heart I'm yielding to Your will the best that I know how." Job submitted himself to God.

Then Job answered the Lord, and said, I know that Thou canst do every thing, and that no thought can be withholden from Thee... Wherefore I abhor myself, and repent in dust and ashes (Job 42:1-2,6).

When Job said that, the peace of God flooded his heart. He was still grief-stricken, to be sure, but he was at peace with God, at peace with the world, and at peace with himself.

Hurt can have a positive or a negative affect upon our lives. Depending on how we respond, it can make us bitter. We can bottle it up on the inside, allowing it to fester like a sore. It should always be remembered that a small wound that becomes infected causes far more pain and is far more troublesome than a large one that heals. If we internalize our hurts, they will sour our personality. Hurt can make us bitter or better.

Retaliate

The second thing that we can do is *retaliate*. We can get even with the people who hurt and offend us. If revenge is what we want most, we can spend the rest of our lives trying to get even. Like toxic waste, revenge will sap your strength and poison your spirit. Retaliation is one of the worst possible ways to handle hurt because it requires time, attention, energy, and effort to carry out. If someone does something that hurts you, you feel that you must do something back. You hurt your offender in order to get even—and the cycle never ends. It was Mahatma Ghandi who said:

"If we insist on living by an eye-for-an-eye kind of justice, the whole world will go blind."

All retaliation ever does is perpetuate evil. There has to be a better way. If revenge is what we want most, we can spend the rest of our lives trying to get even. We will have to stoop to the same level as our offender by violating God's laws and usurping God's authority to administer justice. God commands us not to do so.

Be not overcome of evil, but overcome evil with good (Romans 12:21).

Countless times, I have had individuals, male and female alike, come to my office totally consumed with the desire to get revenge on someone who has abused them in some way. Many times church people cover up these feelings, but they become evident when I listen to the anger and the vehemence with which they speak when they talk about the individual who wronged them. It is human nature to want your offender to feel the same depth of hurt that you feel. However, as I said before, retaliation takes time, effort, and energy. It can be an exhausting enterprise, and the personal price that you pay is not worth your time and effort. You should never give anyone that much power over you.

I often tell people who are trying to cope with separation and divorce that the best revenge is to get healthy physically and spiritually so that you can go on with your life. Do your crying at home. Scream in a pillow. Have a full-scale pity party if you must. Then pull yourself together.

Encourage yourself like David. I have used Psalm 37 so much as a way to encourage myself that I finally committed it to memory. Now when my offenders see me, I am walking tall, shoulders squared, and I have a smile on my face, joy in my heart, and a certain bounce in my step that says, "God and I have everything under control." The best way to retaliate is to become healthy and whole. These are some ways that you can regain your self-confidence and encourage yourself:

- Read Psalms that encourage.
- Compliment yourself.
- Maintain your weight.
- Set aside private prayer time.
- Get enough sleep.
- Build a support network.
- Quit trying to "fix" others.
- Praise others.
- Buy a flower. Smell it.
- Ask a friend for a hug.

It is said that the grizzly bear can terrorize any animal in the West. But there is one animal that the grizzly will allow to eat with him even though he resents the intrusion—the skunk. The grizzly deeply resents the skunk's intrusion, but it has decided that it would be better to find a way to coexist with the skunk than to pay the high price of getting even. Don't retaliate when someone hurts you. All you will succeed in doing is creating a stink.

Forgive

The third thing we can do is *forgive* those who have hurt us, whether they ask for it or not. Moving from the theological to the practical, Paul gives us guidelines for living as a redeemed people in a fallen world. We must learn to live our faith each day, especially during those times when others hurt and offend us.

> *Recompense to no man evil for evil…. If it be possible, as much as lieth in you, live peaceably with all men. …avenge not yourselves, but rather give place unto wrath: for it is written, Vengeance is mine; I will repay, saith the Lord* (Romans 12:17-19).

In this day of constant lawsuits and incessant demands for legal rights, Paul's command sounds impossible. When someone hurts you deeply, instead of giving him what he deserves, Paul says to befriend him:

Therefore if thine enemy hunger, feed him; if he thirst, give him drink: for in so doing thou shalt heap coals of fire on his head (Romans 12:20).

By giving an enemy a drink, we are not excusing his misdeeds. We are recognizing them, forgiving them, and loving the individual in spite of himself—just as Christ did in our case. Why does Paul tell us to forgive our enemies?

1. Forgiveness may break a cycle of retaliation and lead to mutual reconciliation.
2. It may make your enemy feel ashamed and cause him to change his ways.
3. By contrast, returning evil for evil hurts you just as much as it hurts your enemy.

Even if your enemy never repents, forgiving him will free you of a heavy load of bitterness.

Forgiveness involves both attitudes and action. If you find it hard to feel forgiving of someone who has hurt you, try acting forgiving. If appropriate, tell that person that you would like to heal your relationship. Many times you will discover that right actions lead to right feelings.

Christ had a lot to say about forgiveness. When Peter asked Him if He thought a person should forgive someone who had wronged him as many as seven times, Jesus answered,

...I say not unto thee, Until seven times: but, Until seventy times seven (Matthew 18:22).

The rabbis taught that Jews should forgive those who had offended them three times. Peter, in trying to be especially generous, asked Jesus if seven (the "perfect" number) was enough times to forgive someone. But Jesus answered, "Seventy times seven," meaning that we should always forgive someone. We should always forgive those who are truly repentant, even when they don't ask for forgiveness. Because God has forgiven all our sins, we should not hold forgiveness from others. Realizing how completely Christ has forgiven us should produce a free and generous attitude of forgiveness toward others. When we do not forgive others, we are setting ourselves outside and above Christ's law of love.

The greatest example of forgiveness, of course, is Jesus Christ. Evil men accused Him falsely, convicted Him unjustly, beat Him unmercifully, mocked Him cruelly, nailed Him to a cross, and hung Him up to die. With blood running down His scourged back, He looked down from the cross at the hostile crowd and prayed:

>...*Father, forgive them; for they know not what they do*... (Luke 23:34).

Not a twinge of bitterness is present in His words, but only the love and forgiveness that were in His heart toward those who had put Him there. What an example! "That was Christ," you say. "Surely He does not expect me to be like that." Yes, He really does. "But you don't know how deeply I've been hurt," you might say. "No one should have to go through what I had to endure." Quite true. I do not know the depth of hurt that you have felt, but Jesus Christ does. He experienced the deepest hurt in every area of His life—and He never offended anyone. Other people have experienced hurt just as badly as you. If they were able to follow Christ's example and forgive, why can't you?

Hooked on a Feeling

One of my church members, a middle-aged lady with four children, came to my office one day for counseling. She was terribly distraught. Her marriage had ended when her husband of 15 years announced that he wanted to pursue a relationship with a woman at his office with whom he had been having an affair. Now divorced for three years, she was facing financial ruin due to her ex-husband's non-payment of child support. Very graphically, she explained how her ex-husband left town and is living the "good life," while leaving her and their four children to struggle and fend for themselves. She came to me, as her pastor, searching for answers.

I immediately began by talking about forgiveness. The mere mention of the word attached to any discussion about her ex-husband made her react as if I had used a four-letter word. She confessed to me that she did not feel like forgiving the person who had injured her and her children. However, no one ever does. If we wait until we *feel like* forgiving an offender, we never will. If we wait until we feel like cleaning out the garage or taking out the trash or changing a dirty diaper, none of these things will ever happen. Forgiveness is not a feeling. It is something we choose to do by an act of the will.

When I asked her what way she felt that I might be able to help she answered, "I don't know where to begin. My pain is so deep, and I am so angry...I feel helpless to change my feelings." "Begin anyway you like," I said. "Just spill it out—whatever is on your mind." Then she blurted out: "I hate my ex-husband Bill so much, I wish he were dead." "You really don't hate him," I tried to assure her "You hate what he has done to you and your life." "But I do," she insisted. Then after summarizing a laundry list of some of the evil things he had done, she asked, "What can I do to get rid of this awful hatred I feel? Should I attend church more regularly? Should I put more money in the offering plate? How do

I get rid of this terrible hate I feel?" I replied, "Attending church more regularly and putting more money in the offering plate may be a good thing to do, but that is not going to solve your problem of hate." "What am I going to do then?" she desperately wanted to know.

I took her to Matthew 6 and read what Jesus said:

For if ye forgive men their trespasses [offenses] *your heavenly Father will also forgive you: but ye forgive not men their trespasses, neither will your Father forgive your trespasses* (Matthew 6:14-15).

"I can't do that," she insisted. "I can't forgive Bill for the terrible things that he has done." "You're using the wrong word," I said. "You can say I *won't* forgive Bill because that's your choice. Forgiving Bill isn't a matter of *can* or *can't*, it's a matter of *will* or *won't*. We choose to forgive or we choose not to forgive. Extending forgiveness or withholding forgiveness is a matter of choice. Either you will forgive Bill because you choose to forgive him, or you won't forgive him because you choose not to do so. The decision to forgive or not to forgive is a decision that you alone must make."

Even though forgiveness is extended by an act of the will in a moment of time, getting over our wounded feelings may take a while. The deeper the hurt, the longer it may take for the wound to heal. Slowly, however, it will. Our emotions do not always keep pace with our will. Sometimes emotions are slow to get the message. They have to be reprogrammed to catch up with what the will has done. During this period, we may have to keep reminding our emotions that we have forgiven the offender for what he has done and that we do not intend to harbor resentment against him anymore. No, he does not even need to apologize. Once we have already extended forgiveness to someone, that is that. After our emotions finally get the message about what our will has done, we will wake up one morning and be able to remember the incident without feeling any pain or desire for revenge. Then we will know that forgiveness is complete. As long as we hope our offender will be miserable in a new marriage or get fired from his job, we know our forgiveness is not complete.

If you want to be relieved of the anger and depression that you feel, you will have to extend forgiveness to those who hurt you. "If you are unwilling to do this," I told the lady in my office, "your hatred will continue." "Forgive Bill just like that?" she asked. "Just like that," I replied. "Just as Christ has forgiven you for the wrongs you have done, you must forgive Bill for the wrongs he has done. What's your decision going to be?" After a long, deadly silence she said, "*I will.*" "Good," I answered. "Now let's tell the Lord that this is what you're going to do." She began by telling the Lord every terrible thing Bill had done with all the sordid details. Then, finally, she got around to saying: "As You have forgiven me, today I also forgive Bill." After she had spoken those words, I actually saw a change in her countenance and facial expression. Her shoulders dropped, her face relaxed from a tight frown, and she began wiping the tears from her eyes.

She looked as if a heavy load had been lifted from her heart, and this was reflected in her body language. "Wow, that really felt good," she remarked. Healing does not always come as quickly or as dramatically as it did for her. However, when we forgive, the healing process can at least begin.

Off the Hook

When we forgive, we are letting our offender "off the hook." We are releasing him from the obligation to repay what he owes—from the need to return what he has stolen, from the need to apologize for what he has promised, from the need to make a wrong right. When we forgive, we choose to give up our grudge despite the severity of the injury we have received. We are not pretending that it did not hurt or that it did not matter. We are simply forgiving what has been done. This simple exercise will help you begin the process of healing:

1. Talk to yourself.
   - Verbally acknowledge every wrong done to you by your offender.
   - Be frank and brutally honest.
   - Acknowledge your hurt and disappointment.
   - Describe your feelings to yourself, and do so in explicit detail.
2. Pronounce a verdict.
   - List the punishments that your offender *deserves*.
   - Make the punishment fit the crime.
3. Think back.
   - Think about how God has forgiven you.
   - Be frank and brutally honest.
4. Ask God to help you.
   - Ask God to help you extend that same forgiveness toward your offender.
   - Ask God to help you change your feelings.
5. Dismiss the charges.
   - Release your offender.
   - File this case away as a valuable "life lesson."

What if you are the one who is asking for forgiveness and the person you have hurt refuses to accept your apology? All you can do is say that you are sorry and ask for forgiveness. God does not hold you responsible for the other person's response. Do not let his or her reaction get you down. Seek forgiveness, forgive yourself, and get on with your life.

Healthy Choice

Forgiveness is an act of the will; it is a clear and deliberate *healthy* choice. This does not mean that we feel any better about the hurt in our lives. Nor does it mean that the damage was not real. Forgiveness means that we have chosen to release our offender from what he owes. Once we have chosen to release our offender from what he owes, the healing process is free to begin. Sometimes forgiveness brings instant release. On other occasions, it takes time for our emotions to catch up with the action that our will has taken. The thing that usually blocks healing from occurring is our refusal to take the first step: We do not grant a judicial pardon to our offender. Once we do this, the healing process will begin automatically.

Some of us say that we are willing to forgive a person for what he has done, but we are unwilling to forget. If we mean by this that we will never stop holding a grudge against the individual for what he has done, then we have not forgiven him at all. Forgiveness does not mean that we will be unable to remember what has happened. How can one forget a lie, a betrayal, a death, or a divorce? Forgiveness does not cause our memory to fail. As long as our mind is clear, we will be able to remember the hurts we received. "Forgetting" the incident means that we have gotten over the pain that it caused; we no longer want our offender to suffer for what he has done to us. We no longer feel resentment toward him or wish him ill.

This does not always mean we will want to reestablish a close relationship or become intimate friends with someone who has betrayed a confidence. Forgiveness does not always reestablish the relationship. Trust has to be earned. Sometimes we have to keep reminding ourselves that we have made the "healthy choice" to forgive our offender. Otherwise, we will be tempted to mull over previous hurts and take our forgiveness back. This will cause the pain to begin all over again.

To a greater degree than most of us think, our physical and emotional health is tied to our willingness to forgive. Sooner or later, you can either allow malice, bitterness, and hatred to take root in your life, or you can forgive the offender and get on with your life. You can forgive the offender, or you can sink into a world of depression and self-pity. You can forgive the offender or you can nurse a grudge. Emotional stress can trigger all kinds of physical problems—high blood pressure, migraine headaches, bleeding ulcers, strokes, depression, and mental illness. Emotions can govern the flow of adrenaline in our blood, affect the secretions of our glands, and cause muscle tension. The physical side effects that arise from emotional stress can range anywhere from the simple act of blushing to heart and respiratory failure or a terrible case of colitis.

When a teenager came home from school one day, his mother was rushing out the door. "Your father is in the hospital," she announced. "What's wrong with him, mom?" the boy inquired. "He has colitis," was her answer. "Who's he been *colliding* with this time?" her son asked. It is a known fact that many illnesses that doctors treat in their offices today are psychosomatic. They are physical illnesses to be sure, but they spring from unresolved emotional conflict in the patient's life. It is not so much what these people are eating, as what's *eating them* that causes their problems. Why not make the "healthy choice" and live?

Making the conscious choice to get healthy will mean work whether we are talking about physical, emotional, or spiritual health. Most healthy, well-toned, agile people with great bodies have a story to tell about the early morning workouts in the gym, sore muscles, and the pain of passing up that hot apple pie with two scoops of vanilla ice cream. It seems almost impossible in the beginning, but determination, consistency, and hard work pay off. Staying physically healthy requires a change in lifestyle that must be maintained over a lifetime.

Likewise, maintaining spiritual health requires a certain lifestyle that must be maintained over the period of your lifetime. It is hard work in the beginning, but the payoff of a balanced, stable emotional and spiritual state and a healthier physical self makes it well worth all the effort. These are a few of the healthy choices that work for me:

- Learn to say "no" more often.
- Avoid negative people.
- Look at problems as challenges.
- Smile.
- Unclutter your life.
- Schedule play time.
- Stop talking negatively.
- Be aware of your decisions.
- Find a "vent partner."
- Remember, stress is an attitude.

A Loser's Game

Hate is a loser's game; a dead-end street leading nowhere. In *None of These Diseases*, Dr. S.I. McMillen said,

"The moment I start hating a man, I become his slave. I can't enjoy my work anymore because he even controls my thoughts. My resentments produce too many stress hormones in my body and I become fatigued after only a few hours of work. The work I used to enjoy is now drudgery. Even vacations don't bring me pleasure because I take my angry thoughts on the road with me. The man I hate hounds me wherever I go...The man I hate may be miles from my bedroom, but more cruel than any slave driver, he whips my thoughts into such a frenzy that my innerspring mattress becomes a rack of torture. I really must acknowledge the fact that I am a slave to every man on whom I pour the viles of my wrath."

Sometimes we feel that our offender does not deserve to be forgiven. Maybe he or she does not, but that is not for us to decide. God has not given us the option of making that judgment. Hatred and bitterness are the venom of life that needs to be removed like a snakebite that has to be slit open and the poison sucked out and spat away. Forgiveness is the healing that draws the poison out. It is cheaper to forgive than to hate. To forgive a wrongdoer for what he has done is to cut a malignancy out of your heart.

The inconsistency of our asking God to forgive us while we remain unwilling to forgive others is an affront to Him. Jesus talked about a man who owed a king a very large debt—10,000 talents (see Mt. 18:22-35). This debt was the equivalence of 15 years of wages. Because the man begged for mercy when the payment was due, the king was moved with compassion and forgave him all of it. However, the same man who had been forgiven such a great amount went out and found a man who owed him 100 denarii—a sum that could be worked off in a day. Because that man could not pay the debt on the spot, the first man ignored his pleas of mercy. When the king heard what this man had done, he became angry. He took back his forgiveness and threw that ungrateful soul into prison until all was paid. God will not forgive our wrongs if we refuse to forgive others their wrongs.

So likewise shall My heavenly Father do also unto you, if ye from your hearts forgive not every one his brother their trespasses (Matthew 18:35).

WRiTiNG IT OFF

Extending forgiveness is difficult. It seems so unnatural, and it is such an expensive thing to do, for the cost is always borne by the one who does the forgiving. If I break an expensive vase of yours and you forgive me, you suffer the loss and I go free. If I ruin your reputation and you forgive me, you bear the hurt and I go free. Forgiveness is taking a note that is owed and canceling it so that nothing remains. The amount that you forgive is the amount you lose. Forgiveness does not restore the goods that were stolen or the marriage that was destroyed or the family that was broken up. It does not repair the damage that was done; it writes it off. The following are some things to remember:

- Any emotion is removable.
- Face negative emotions head-on.
- Resolve to be a person of faith.

Any Emotion Is Removable

Anger is removable, hatred is removable, and depression is removable. The first step in overcoming any negative emotion is simply to realize that it is, for a fact, removable. Never entertain the fact that you must live with a negative emotion all your life. Eleanor Roosevelt said, "You gain strength, courage and confidence by every experience by which you really stop to look anger, fear and unforgiveness in the face." When a person determinedly stands up to something, that something tends to finally fold and give way. There is much less danger in standing up to a difficulty or fear than in trying to avoid or run away from it.

Face Negative Emotions Head-On

An old deacon in my church once shared with me that he had learned life's most important lesson from Hereford cows. Growing up in the country, he had worked on farms all his life where winter storms took a heavy toll on the cattle. Freezing wind and rains whipped across the open fields. Howling, bitter winds piled snow into huge drifts. Temperatures dropped below zero for days on end. Flying ice cut into the flesh. In this maelstrom of nature's violence, most cattle turned their backs to the icy blasts and slowly drifted downwind, mile upon mile. They would finally come up against a boundary fence. There, they would pile up against the barrier and die by the scores.

But the Herefords acted differently. Cattle of this breed would instinctively head into the windward end of the range. There they would stand shoulder-to-shoulder, facing the storm's blast, heads down against its onslaughts. "You most always found the Herefords alive and well," said the deacon. "I guess that is the greatest lesson I ever learned on the farm—just face life's difficulties and storms head-on."

Resolve To Be a Person of Faith

In canceling out negative emotions, the number one thing to do is say determinedly:

"I do not want to be motivated by unforgiveness, anger, and hurt anymore. I don't want to be dominated by these emotions. I now decide—I now determine—I now will—that my negative emotions be brought under control, even eliminated, and that I will become a person of faith."

Of course, saying these things, however strongly, will not in itself accomplish them; but they will be accomplished when you strongly affirm them and determine to make your desire and decision really stick. Adopt a method of increasing faith quickly. It works! In the best sense, faith is the result of a long-developing spiritual process. But since we have the practical problem of dealing with unforgiveness and hurt and just haven't the faith to counteract it, we are left with the necessity for building faith up at once. To do this, I suggest taking large "doses" of faith into your mind. Work at it zealously and constantly, with the definite purpose of saturating your very consciousness. Search the Scriptures for passages that express the greatest values people have ever had. Commit these to memory. Say them over and over until they completely dominate your thinking. It will not be very long until these powerful "faith thoughts" begin to displace your fears.

Two Faith Thoughts

I sought the Lord and He heard me and delivered me from all my fears (Psalm 34:4).

To say, "I sought the Lord" means that I really determined to find Him and that this very determination brought me to Him.

I will fear no evil: for Thou art with me (Psalm 23:4).

Get the presence of God fixed in your mind and negative emotions will fade away.

The story is told of two men who traveled through life with sacks on their backs. Each time a hurt was received, they would place it in what became known as their "injury sack." One man's sack became so bulging and heavy that he could not walk without difficulty or pain. The other man's sack was empty and light. There was nothing in it. "How can your 'injury sack' be empty?" a stranger asked. "Have you never been hurt?" "Oh yes, I have been hurt many times," the man replied, "As my sack grew large and its weight became unbearable, I asked a friend one day if he would help me carry the load. 'No one can help you carry the load of hurt,' he replied, 'but there is a way for you to rid yourself of it. Take the scissors of forgiveness and slit the bottom of your sack. Then your load of hurt will fall away.' That is what I chose to do that day. Since then, I take all hurts that I receive and place them into my 'injury sack' as before, but now they simply slide out the bottom. That is one load I choose not to carry."

The decision is yours to make. You can go through life carrying a load of unforgiveness in your heart with all the resentment, depression, anxiety, cynicism, and emotional fallout that it brings, or you can forgive your offender as Christ forgave His offenders.

Then said Jesus, Father, forgive them; for they know not what they do... (Luke 23:34).

To forgive or not to forgive—that is a decision that you alone can make. Pray this prayer to begin to reprogram your mind and encourage your heart to forgive your offender:

Lord, I acknowledge my pain, hurt, and feeling of betrayal. Help me to forgive _____ as God has also forgiven me. Draw out the poison of bitterness and resentment. Remove my desire for revenge. Replace it with the love of Christ. Thank You for Your healing in this area of my life. Amen.

CHAPTER 6

Dessert

*We took sweet counsel together, and walked unto
the house of God in company* (Psalm 55:14).

My 80-year-old Aunt Francis always urged the children to eat sparingly of the main course in order to leave a little room for the "hereafter." A good dessert after a good meal can indeed be heavenly. Desserts give the hostess a chance to produce a startling soufflé, an extraordinary cake, or a mouth-watering, knee-slapping sweet potato pie. I always had a difficult time pacing myself during the main course of the meal because there were always so many foods to choose from that I loved. Tempting as the desserts were, I was usually not able to settle down and enjoy the dessert portion of the meal until hours after the dishes were done and the kitchen was shut down because I was too full. But the wait was always worthwhile.

Aunt Francis could bake pies and cakes like "nobody's business." She always boasted about her secret ingredients and the little special touches that she hid in tin cans that used to make her desserts a lasting memory. I looked in those cans many times. They were just spices and things. I realize now that it was the combination, the measurement and the mixture of what my aunt used that made her cakes and pies so special and not just the ingredients themselves.

I laugh now when I think about my first taste of a "box" cake. I was at a friend's house. Her mom had just returned from the supermarket with bags of groceries filled to the brim. My friend and I were excited as we unpacked the bags and put the items in their proper places. Then my friend's mother began to prepare dinner. I was invited. All the familiar items that I saw in my own home every week were there—fatback, seasoning, milk, cheese, macaroni, and sweet potatoes. Then my friend's mother began to tell us about a special cake that she wanted us to help her prepare for dessert. My mouth watered, and my stomach grumbled as she asked us to choose from a selection of frostings. The vote was unanimous—vanilla frosting and coconut.

After the meat was seasoned and placed in the oven and the vegetables were well on their way it was time to make the dessert. I was waiting to see the old familiar spoon, bowl, eggs, sugar, and heavy cream appear from the refrigerator and cupboard. Instead, a bowl, a box, a mixer, and a cup of water stood on the table. I knew that people made cakes from boxes of mix, but I had never seen it done before. The women in my family made everything from scratch. The preparation of the cake took a total of ten minutes. No sooner than the box had been opened, the batter was being poured into a cake pan and shoved into the oven.

The dinner my friend's mom prepared was quite good, but the dessert left much to be desired. Dessert should be something that one looks forward to. A good dessert that delights the palate and adds the perfect finishing touch to an extraordinary meal should take time to prepare. Careful, thoughtful preparation ensures maximum enjoyment. Anything that is truly enjoyable is worthy of the time and preparation necessary to make the experience exceptional.

This "dessert chapter" provides the finishing touch to the inspirational, spiritual meal that has gone before. Time, careful thought, prayer, and preparation have gone into these conclusions. Like sopping up the gravy of what is left over from a wonderful piece of meat, these reflections will add insight and inspiration to situations that you encounter every day. Some of these reflections are profound, while others are more obvious and easily understood. This is also how some desserts are: Some are rich and heavy and ladened with calories like hot apple cobbler with homemade vanilla ice cream, while other desserts are just coffee and tea or a flavored sparkling water. Regardless of what it is, a good dessert should provide the final comment to a fabulous meal.

God's Invitation

Gods gives each of us an open invitation to get to know Him personally.

All things are delivered unto Me of My Father: and no man knoweth the Son, but the Father; neither knoweth any man the Father, save the Son, and he to whomsoever the Son will reveal Him (Matthew 11:27).

In the Old Testament, "know" means more than knowledge. It implies intimate relationship. The communion between God the Father and God the Son is the core of Their relationship. For anyone else to know God, God must reveal Himself to that person by the Son's choice. How blessed we are that Jesus has clearly revealed to us God, His truth, and how we can know Him.

God gives each of us an open invitation to learn about Him.

Take My yoke upon you, and learn of Me; for I am meek and lowly in heart: and ye shall find rest unto your souls. For My yoke is easy, and My burden is light (Matthew 11:29-30).

A yoke is a heavy wooden harness that fits over the shoulders of an ox or set of oxen. It is attached to a piece of equipment that the oxen are to pull. A person may be carrying the heavy burdens of sin, betrayal, bitterness, fear, doubt, worry, oppression, persecution, or just weariness of life. Jesus frees people from all these burdens when they learn of Him and His willingness and availability to help them. The "rest" Jesus promises is love, healing, and peace with God. It is not the end of all effort. A relationship with God changes meaningless toil into spiritual productivity and purpose.

We come to know God intimately and personally through prayer and a sincere study of His Word. The Word of God is like the "dessert" of life because it gives the final comment that tells us what life is all about. God's invitation to us to get "up close and personal" with Him is not extended to any other part of His creation. A true understanding of God's Word "sweetens" even the most bitter experiences of life because the Word brings understanding. The Word of God is special. It cannot be compared to any other book written or conceived in the human mind.

I often tell my church members that you cannot read a verse of Scripture a day, with no spiritual insight or guidance, and expect to gain an understanding of God's Word. I always know who the "serious saints" are by their level of commitment to Bible study and their interest in studying God's Word. "A person who is *really* interested in establishing an intimate relationship with God does not have a laundry list of ready-made excuses as to why they do not attend Bible study," I always say. When two people are interested in pursuing a relationship, they adjust their schedules and do whatever is necessary in order to spend quality and quantity time with each other. The same is true with God. We cannot expect to "know" God when we spend no quality or quantity of time with Him.

It is not enough to merely read the Word of God like some ritual. One must read with understanding, and in order to do so, one must be consistently taught. Disciplining oneself to study the Word of God is one of the most difficult areas of our Christian growth. Yet we cannot grow without it. The Word of God is special; it should be handled with care. What an abomination it is to allow something so sweet and precious to lie on a living room coffee table and gather dust.

The whole Bible is God's inspired Word. Because it is inspired and trustworthy, we should *read it* and *apply it* to our lives. The Bible is our standard for testing everything else that claims to be true. It is our source of guidance for how we should live. God wants to show you what is true and equip you to live for Him.

All scripture is given by inspiration of God, and is profitable for doctrine, for reproof, for correction, for instruction in righteousness (2 Timothy 3:16).

I am constantly amazed at how relevant the Word of God is to our modern-day situations. There is truly nothing new under the sun (see Eccles. 1:9). Every area of human drama and interaction can be found in Scripture, as well as God's answer to every situation. For example, Proverbs gives practical suggestions for effective living. This book is not just a collection of homey sayings; it contains deep spiritual insights drawn from experience. The Book of Proverbs focuses on God—His character, works, and blessings—and it tells how we can live in close relationship with Him.

To know wisdom and instruction; to perceive the words of under-standing ... The fear of the Lord is the beginning of knowledge... (Proverbs 1:2,7a).

It grieves my spirit to see people in church dealing with heartbreaking situations, knowing that their misery is prolonged because they will not go to God through His Word to get answers and direction. Pastors see this phenomena all the time in counseling sessions with distraught individuals. Hurting people want a "quick fix" and "quick answers" to problems that often took years to develop. When I suggest that they begin to seriously study God's Word in addition to seeking whatever else is needed for total healing, such as medical services or professional counseling, they look at me with disdain. But there is no getting away from the truth of the need for the guidance of God's Word in our lives.

God is more than willing to pour out His wisdom to us. To receive His advice, we must be willing to listen and refuse to let pride cause us to think more highly of our own wisdom and desires than God's. If we think we know better than God, or if we feel that we have no need of God's direction, we have fallen into foolish pride. In the Book of Proverbs, a fool is not described as someone with a mental deficiency, but as someone with a character deficiency (such as rebellion, laziness, anger). The fool is not stupid, but he is unable to tell right from wrong or good from bad.

How long, ye simple ones [fools] *will ye love simplicity? And the scorners delight in their scorning, and fools hate knowledge? Turn you at my reproof: behold, I will pour out my spirit unto you, I will make known my words unto you* (Proverbs 1:22-23).

He that refuseth instruction despiseth his own soul: but he that heareth reproof getteth understanding. The fear of the Lord is the instruction of wisdom; and before honour is humility (Proverbs 15:32-33).

If you do not want to learn, years of schooling will teach you very little. But if you want to be taught, there is no end to what you can learn. This includes being willing to accept correction and to learn from the wisdom of God and others. A person who refuses godly instruction has a problem with pride. Such a person is unlikely to learn very much. In our zeal for the truth and wisdom of Scripture, we must never forget its purpose—to help us to know God, to develop an intimate relationship with Him, to give direction for our lives, and to equip us to do good for others. We should not study God's Word simply to increase our own knowledge or to prepare us to win arguments. We should study and obey Scripture so that we will know who God is. Our knowledge of God's Word is useless unless it points us to a deeper intimacy with Him.

Respond to God's invitation. Get to know Him personally. Learn about Him by studying His Word. Join a Bible study group. Allow God's guidance to sweeten your bitter experiences. The following qualities describe how you should read the Bible:

1. Frequently, daily (Josh. 1:8).
2. Not for controversy, but for your profit (Prov. 3).
3. Meditatively (Ps. 1:2).
4. In love (Ps. 119:97-104).
5. With consciousness of need (Mt. 5:6; Jn. 7:37-39; 2 Pet. 1:1-10; 3:18).
6. In faith (Rom. 10:17; Heb. 11:6).
7. Searchingly (Jn. 5:39).
8. Open to its work (Heb. 4:12; Jude 3).
9. By comparing Scripture with Scripture (1 Cor. 2:13).
10. In the Spirit (Jn. 14:16-18; 15:26).

Better Than a Therapist's Couch

The Word of God is better than a therapist's couch. The therapist listens to the details of an individual's life. There is an exchange of theories, opinions, and ideas. The therapist acts as an advisor to the patient, but in and of him or herself, the therapist has no healing or curative powers. The Word of God, on the other hand, is more than a theory or idea. God's Word is not just information; it is for our transformation. Becoming a believer means beginning a whole new relationship with God, not just turning over a new leaf or determining to do right. Believers have a changed purpose, direction, attitude, and behavior.

Jesus opened people's minds to understand the Scriptures. The Holy Spirit does this in our lives today when we study the Bible.

Then opened He [Jesus] *their understanding, that they might understand the scriptures* (Luke 24:45).

Have you ever wondered how to understand a difficult Bible passage? Besides reading surrounding passages, asking other people, and consulting reference works, pray that the Holy Spirit will open your mind to understand, giving you the needed insight to put God's Word into action in your life.

Our lives are cluttered with rule books, but the authors never come with us to help us follow the rules. God, however, does. That is the uniqueness of our Bible. God not only provides the rules and the guidelines, but He also comes along with us personally each day to help us live according to those rules. All we must do is invite Him and respond to His direction. Almost any long trip requires a map or guide. As we travel through life, the Bible should be our road map, pointing out safe routes, obstacles to avoid, and our final destination. We must recognize ourselves as pilgrims or travelers here on earth who need to study God's map. Otherwise, we will wander aimlessly through life and risk missing our real destination.

God's Word makes us wise. True wisdom goes beyond amassing knowledge, it is *applying* knowledge in a life-changing way. Wisdom comes from allowing what God teaches to guide us. To walk safely in the woods at night, we need a light to avoid tripping over tree roots or falling into holes. In this life, we walk through a dark forest of evil and all types of unexpected situations. But the Bible can be our light to show us the way ahead so that we won't stumble as we walk. It reveals the entangling roots of false values and philosophies.

Through Thy precepts I get understanding: therefore I hate every false way. Thy Word is a lamp unto my feet, and a light unto my path (Psalm 119:104-105).

Life must be lived and experienced, not feared and dreaded. One cannot live life to its fullest without the guidance of God's Word. Pray this prayer to gain understanding of the Bible.

Lord, make plain Your precepts. Open my mind and understanding to Your Word. Help me live according to Your rules and to respond to Your direction. Help me to develop a love and respect for Your Word as I follow You. Amen.

This book is not meant to be "pocket therapy"—a book that offers tips to stressed-out readers for easing their nerves. Nor does this book endeavor to give instant answers or quick fixes for life's most complex and profound problems. What it has promised to do is bring into focus the fuzzy areas of life that keep us asking God, "Why? What does this mean?" The key to inner peace and the answers to every question anyone could ever ask about life are found within the pages of the Holy Scriptures.

Sweetening Your Life

If you "digest" God's Word, you will find that not only does it make you stronger in your faith, but its wisdom "sweetens" your life. You must feed yourself spiritually, just as you do physically. This means doing more than simply giving God's message a casual glance. You must make digesting God's Word a regular part of your life. Belief in God and following His Word is not a crutch for those too weak to stand on their own. God makes us strong enough to stand against anything or anyone, including those who hate what is right. God wants to give you the stability, perseverance, and insight you need to live up to the great task that He has given you. Give yourself over to a serious study of God's Word, and let Him get your life in shape.

In order for our life to be "sweetened," we must not only know the Scriptures; we must also live by them. Jesus exposed the hypocritical attitudes of the religious leaders. They knew the Scriptures, but they did not live by them. They did not care about *being* holy, just in *looking* holy in order to receive the people's admiration and praise:

> *But all their works they do for to be seen of men... Ye serpents, ye generation of vipers, how can ye escape the damnation of hell?* (Matthew 23:5,33).

Today, like the religious leaders of Jesus' day, there are many people who know the Bible but do not let it change their lives. They say that they follow Jesus, but they do not live by His standards. People who live this way are hypocrites. We must make sure our actions match our beliefs. Sometimes people do not believe that God is active in this world, so they do not expect to be changed or transformed. Often we run into people who are looking for God among the dead, just as the women did who brought spices to the tomb of Jesus (see Lk. 24). They study the Bible as a mere historical document and go to church as if to a memorial service. But Jesus is not among the dead—He is alive! Look for signs of His power in your life; they are all around you. Pray this prayer.

> *Lord, change and transform my life through Your Word. Make me more sensitive to Your power and presence around me. Allow me to digest Your Word so that it nourishes my soul and strengthens my daily walk. Allow the Word to sweeten the bitter circumstances of my life. Amen.*

Food For Thought

Real life is the collision—day in and day out—of the improbable with the impossible. We can better handle life's impossible situations by being prepared with enough wisdom from the Word of God so that we can learn from our experiences. Just as dough rises in a bowl, expanding before it becomes bread, we become larger than we thought possible when we rise to occasions by looking past the pain of heartbreaking experiences to see the valuable lessons that they can teach us.

Jesus tells us that in spite of the inevitable struggles we all face, we are not alone.

...In the world ye shall have tribulation: but be of good cheer; I have overcome the world (John 16:33).

Jesus does not abandon us to our struggles either. If we remember that the ultimate victory has already been won, we can claim the peace of Christ in the most troublesome times. Going through rivers of difficulty will either cause you to drown or force you to grow stronger. If you go in your own strength, you are more likely to drown. If you invite the Lord to go with you, He will protect you because God is by nature a Savior, both temporarily and eternally.

When thou passest through the waters, I will be with thee; and through the rivers, they shall not overflow thee: when thou walkest through the fire, thou shalt not be burned; neither shall the flame kindle upon thee (Isaiah 43:2).

Life is a struggle—a bittersweet struggle. There is a current that is always against you because we live in a fallen world. Even though we can have big fun along the way, we were not sent here to play. In Ecclesiastes, Solomon shows us that we should enjoy life, but this does not exempt us from obeying God's commands. We should search for purpose and meaning in life, but they cannot be found in human endeavors. We should acknowledge the evil, foolishness, and injustice in life, yet maintain a positive attitude and strong faith in God.

Life is not a dress rehearsal. Some of us have a utopian idea of what our lives should be. We want all our days to run smoothly and our relationships to be without complication, but that is not life. It is not the truth about what this journey has been for anyone passing through—including Jesus. We have all been sent this way for a purpose. We are here at this time and place because we have lessons to learn and contributions to make. Life is work! If the truth be told, life is uncertain. Anything can happen along the way, but once examined in a divine light, what happens can move us toward enlightenment and personal growth.

Our lives are filled with people and circumstances that are not of our choosing but were given to us by God to aid our growth. All of life's struggles and challenges are custom-designed by God to build character in us and to teach us virtues that we could not learn otherwise. Life was never intended to be a smooth ride. The bumps and thumps and crooked places along the way cause us to slow down and navigate carefully. In our slowing down, we look at certain things that otherwise would go unnoticed if the journey were smooth and swift. Paul encouraged Timothy to endure hardness and suffering because his struggles better prepared him for his ministry by building character, discipline, and endurance.

Thou therefore endure hardness, as a good soldier of Jesus Christ. ... If we suffer, we shall also reign with Him... (2 Timothy 2:3,12).

Have you ever studied a diamond? It is radiantly beautiful from all angles, yet it is strong enough to withstand the assaults of time. Nothing compares to the lasting brilliance of a diamond. For example, I received an engagement ring from a man whom I believed would be the prince charming that all little girls grow up thinking that they will meet. He turned out to be a frog, but the diamond ring never lost its luster and hardness. Our faith and dependence upon God are to be like that diamond—intact and strong enough to withstand the dissappointments of life.

The Pie of Discontent

Every one of us takes a bite out of the *pie of discontent* at one time or another. Some situations look good on the outside, only to prove to be a big disappointment later. I once asked my great-grandmother, who was born around 1890, how she was able to handle the hard times of growing up in the racist South and being limited in life because she was a "colored" woman. She said in a soft, hushed voice, "I could hate life and hate people, but I'd rather think about Jesus. Even when they nailed His hands and feet, He was loving. It helps to think about that when going through hard times."

Paul reminds us that even though we may be at the end of our rope, we are never at the end of hope.

We are troubled on every side, yet not distressed; we are perplexed, but not in despair; persecuted, but not forsaken; cast down, but not destroyed (2 Corinthians 4:8-9).

Our perishable bodies are subject to sin and suffering, but God never abandons us. All our problems, humiliations, and trials are opportunities for Christ to demonstrate His power and presence through us and to give us inner peace. Paul faced sufferings, trials, and distress as he preached the gospel. But he knew that they would one day be over and that he would obtain God's rest and rewards. As we face great troubles, it is easy to focus on the pain that we are experiencing now, rather than the ultimate goal. Just as athletes concentrate on the finish line and ignore their discomfort, we too must focus on the reward we receive for our faith, like strength and the joy that lasts forever.

For all things are for your sakes, that the abundant grace might through the thanksgiving of many rebound to the glory of God. For which cause we faint not; but though our outward man perish, yet the inward man is renewed day by day. For our light affliction which is but for a moment, worketh for us a far more exceeding and eternal weight of glory (2 Corinthians 4:15-17).

No matter what happens to us in this life, we have the assurance of eternal life when suffering will end. Pray this prayer to help you renew your strength and maintain inner peace when you are going through trials:

Lord, increase my strength. Increase my level of endurance. When persecution wears me down, help me to concentrate on the inner strength that the Holy Spirit gives me. Help me to stay in the race and keep my eyes focused on the goal of living a life of triumph and obedience to You. Comfort me in times of stress. Give me peace when I feel defeated. Help me to experience the joy that transcends everything that I'm going through. Amen.

Maintaining Inner Peace

Maintaining inner peace should be a conscious daily goal. You can develop an exercise of affirmation and healthy "self talk" to encourage you. Today my life is more settled than it ever was—it's more on an even keel because I have found inner peace. My inner peace comes from my ability to see life from God's perspective. I have learned God's perspective of my life through a consistent, serious study of God's Word. Through the study of God's Word, I can hear His voice in my spirit. I can also hear the wise counsel of the ancient women who gather in my thoughts to give me advice and guidance. They give me counsel and advise me every time I think about the wisdom and good advice they so willingly shared. Those women suffered through peril that I will never encounter. They not only survived; they thrived. Now, I realize how strong I am because I am made of the same "stuff."

I know that I will never have everything I want in my life. But in each holy moment I have everything I need to experience the joy of living. As we mature, we must learn how important it is to continuously ask ourselves, *Who am I? What lessons must I learn from the upheaval in my life?* Every hurt and every struggle is God's invitation to grow. Our crises can catalyze real transformation. All the things that seem devastating are for our growth, never our punishment. They are meant to tear down old structures so that we can build new and better functioning ones. When we view life through this prism, we will look at the world with quiet eyes. Those quiet eyes are the rest and peace we feel during turbulent times.

Learn to form healthy habits by rehearsing Scripture to encourage yourself. Recruit your body to be a servant to the spiritual man. One of my favorite passages of the Bible is Psalm 23. My mother made me learn it years ago, and it has stayed with me. Mothers can do that—give a child something to hold on to or a new way to see the world. I will never forget it. It is important to make special memories with the people you love. Everyday life fades from your mind, but it is easy to remember the celebrations and the good times. Those memories linger like the sweetness of chocolate long after a last bite of cake has found its final resting place.

I cannot recall all those conversations I had with the older women in my family on ordinary evenings, but I do remember vividly the Christmases and birthdays and weddings and funerals that I spent with my mother, grandmothers, and aunts. Family is the greatest blessing of this life. It is the vehicle by which we pass on whatever tools we have to help our children get the most out of life. When I was a young child, Psalm 23 had little meaning for me. It was just another one of many Scriptures that my mother made me learn. Now that I am older, that psalm has taken on a totally new meaning for me. Reciting this portion of Scripture while I was going through a particularly difficult time helped me learn to encourage myself. Over the years I have memorized many more such passages. In order to recruit your body to be a servant to the spiritual man do the following:

1. Present your body to God daily as a living sacrifice.
2. Conform to the things of God.
3. Don't talk doubt and unbelief.
4. Praise God every day.
5. Be kind to yourself. Say encouraging things.

Our Great Blessing

Self-awareness, which is a great blessing, is also the source of much of our pain and frustration. Our lives can become a painful journey due to our emotional responses to challenge and change. The frustration we feel is often caused by our misperception of life. We give false value to our feelings and experiences. We separate them into categories and label them good or bad. Therefore, loss of any kind—the loss of a loved one, health, a relationship, a job, a treasured possession—devastates us. Loss is a challenge for us to grow and learn and hopefully become better individuals.

Anything that can happen eventually will. And many things that we would not choose for ourselves will happen to us. In fear of this reality, we spend our whole lives running from pain and pursuing pleasure. But neither is permanent—neither the sorrow nor the joy. Life is fleeting, a forever-changing scene, and all our experiences are valuable. That is why it is so important that we pass them on. When we learn to embrace with all our might this difficult aspect of the human experience, then will we surrender joyfully to God.

Personal Dramas

Listen to your life. It is the most important work of your lifetime. Know what is working well for you and what is missing. Be aware of *where* and *why* you may be hurting or feeling unfulfilled. Become aware of what you need to release and what you need to gain more of.

Spending quiet time alone gives your mind an opportunity to renew itself and create order. This can be a difficult but necessary task in such a hurried world.

Through solitude and reflection, you will discover the meaning of life and learn the value of each of your experiences. Taking time to examine your life makes you conscious of what is true for you and valuable for you. You become more accepting of your uniqueness and gain a greater understanding of how important you are to God. The leader of your country probably does not know you by name, let alone think about you. But the King of all creation, the Ruler of the universe, is thinking about you right now. Allow this truth to buoy your self-esteem. If God always has us in His thoughts, perhaps we could do more to keep Him in our thoughts.

But I am poor and needy; yet the Lord thinketh upon me... (Psalm 40:17).

Quiet reflection encourages personal growth. You become aware of how to soothe and heal yourself. To settle for unhappiness in any area of our lives is to miss the whole purpose of living. We can even find happiness in a difficulty or a tragedy when we are able to look beyond the situation itself to see the greater *lesson* that it will teach us. The personal dramas that make us anxious are God's way of encouraging us to reach, to stretch, to grow. Life gives us the exercises to develop wisdom, faith, courage, strength, and hope.

The ART of Living

If we are not present in our lives, or if we resist the lessons that life is trying to teach us, we will settle for a job, a relationship, or a state of mental or physical health that makes us feel miserable. When we are present in our lives, we are sensitive, tuned in, and responsive to the lessons that life can teach us. People who are always angry about something usually blame others for their problems. It is the unsupportive partner, the dysfunctional family they were raised in, the insecure boss, the sexism, the racism—always something outside of themselves that is making them unhappy. People who are always miserable have invested their time in holding on to their pain. Acknowledging the fact that we all have difficult situations in our lives is one of the hurdles that we must jump over to create our own happiness. There is an art to living. There is an art to creating our own joy and happiness. We must listen to our lives. Otherwise, we will keep repeating the same mistakes and finding ourselves in the same painful situations. Remember these key points:

- Listen to your life.
- Find solitude.
- Honestly examine your life.

The very thing that we fear is what we need more of: solitude. Some people overbook their time and over schedule their life in order to avoid too much time alone with themselves. It is necessary for us to create space in our lives where we are still and silent, without the television or stereo blasting, without chatting on the phone. We need quiet time to examine our lives openly and honestly, without feeling defensive or guilty. We must take off our masks, lay down our armor, and put aside our roles, our possessions, and our pretentions so that we can be naked with ourselves.

CReaTe Life

We can struggle through life without ever doing the things that will make us happy and healthy, the things that will ensure that our personal relationships are fulfilling. We know, for instance, that in order to have healthy, mutually satisfying relationships, we need to plan to surround ourselves with healthy, well-rounded people. How often have I heard countless women complain that there are no "good men" left. Their biological time clock is not ticking louder; it is not ticking at all. The clock is broken because they are over 30, and there is no one suitable in sight. The tragedy is that the answer to many of life's dilemmas lies within us. With the leading of the Holy Spirit, we create the life we live through the choices and decisions we make.

I say to women: "You can create better opportunities for yourself in any area of endeavor if you are willing to commit yourself to work harder." You may need to spend more time on personal care and spiritual development, learn new skills, or join new groups of people. In other words, you must be committed to managing your life instead of leaving crucial areas to chance.

Life is short no matter how long we live. If there is something important that you want to do, do not put it off for a better day because that elusive "better day" never comes. Ask yourself, "If I had only six months to live, what would I do, where would I go, who would I spend it with?" Tell someone that you love him or her. Deal with an undisciplined area in your life. Tell someone about Jesus. Since life is short, don't neglect what is truly important. Let the final comments on your life be sweet ones.

God's Wisdom

Everything has its own uniqueness. At some point, you have to stop and appreciate God's wisdom in making you exactly as He did. As a child, it was utterly fascinating for me to learn that God never makes two raindrops, two leaves, or two blades of grass exactly alike. Each thing has its own uniqueness and manifests the magnificent wisdom of the Creator. None of us can undo what we have failed to do or revisit the things that we could have done better. But we can lead our children and others to the path of God. Once another person finds God, it eliminates all the excuses about having parents who did not do all they should have or all they could have. When you have a personal, intimate relationship with God, the past becomes less important because you can remake yourself into His image. This truth is the great healing balm for anyone who has experienced failure in life. You cannot hold on to weaknesses and become strong. But if you can face your weaknesses and overcome them, then you can share your solutions with someone else who is struggling and help them to overcome theirs. Through fellowship and relationship with God, you will come away with the *clear understanding* that you can be your own best friend or your own worst enemy. Stop blaming and start learning from others and start to get out of the way of your own progress.

Sweet Endings

I can still see my great-grandmother sitting on the front porch quitely peeling an apple as the traffic of the city roared by. She didn't enjoy those "new-fangled desserts" as she called them, like lemon meringue pie, chocolate mousse, and cherries jubilee. "Just give me a simple, sweet apple" she would say, "or a green one with a little salt; that's a dessert too," and she would have a sweet ending to a good meal. I cherish my grandmother's simple ways and basic, godly wisdom. It has guided me through the complexities of a life that she never knew. Yet her simple wisdom, which was based on the Word of God, is valuable and relevant just the same. I did not feel that way in my younger years because sometimes her words seemed harsh. But now that I am older, her words are sweeter and more palatable because I have heard them in my thoughts often enough and seen their value. Like my grandmother's salted green apples, if you eat them often enough, the bitterness becomes palatable.

We must do for others, especially younger people, what our elders did for us. They *cleared a path* and made a way for us by sharing their wisdom instead of taking it to the graveyard with them. Many of those ancient, godly women lie in unmarked graves, as if their lives never happened. But those women *did* exist, and they live on in the stories that they left behind and in the memories of those of us whose lives have been enriched by their telling of them. If we stop passing on our stories, this generation will grow up without them. In those stories are the symbols, the images, the metaphors, and the godly wisdom that must be passed down so that our children will not grow up empty. We must practice opening our hearts wider. There are no quick fixes. But the mere fact that our grandmothers discovered their power and worth without the dollars or the technology we now have at our disposal merely by encouraging and sharing what they knew with one another, should assure us that we can discover our own power and worth as well.

Our greatest challenges are to remember who we are—the people who refused to die—and to do the work. Each of us is unique, sent forth with everything we need to live fully and freely and make our special contribution. But many of us live and die with our song unsung, our music trapped in our throat, because we do not understand how important we are to God and because we do not see our innate power and beauty. We are too busy measuring ourselves against each other and valuing the external over the eternal. Purpose in your heart to react positively to every situation that you encounter in your life because there are lessons in the leftovers—then pass them on!

Chapter 7

Cleaning Up and Putting Things Away

*Holding forth the word of life; that I may rejoice
in the day of Christ, that I have not run in vain,
neither laboured in vain* (Phillipians 2:16).

At the end of any good meal, an unpleasant yet necessary process begins. It is time to clean things up and put them away. Everything has its proper place. It is important that pots, pans, dishes, and utensils that were used in the preparation, presentation, and participation of the meal be put back in their proper place so that they will be readily available when they are needed again. Now that you have come to the end of this spiritual meal, an unpleasant yet necessary process must also begin. Now that you have been nourished and nurtured by the spiritual food on these pages, you must allow the truth of God's Word to "clean up" different areas of your life. Ponder those things in your heart, Solomon says:

Ponder the path of thy feet, and let all thy ways be established. Turn not to the right hand nor to the left: remove thy foot from evil (Proverbs 4:26-27).

Examine, study, contemplate, scrutinize, reflect, investigate, and prayerfully consider the truth of God's Word in your heart. To a great extent, our heart— our feelings of love and desire— dictates how we live because we always find time to do what we enjoy. Solomon tells us to keep our heart with all digilence, making sure that we concentrate on those desires that will keep us on the right path. Make sure that your affections push you in the right direction. Put boundaries on your desires. When you are faced with a decision that will have a lasting effect and great impact upon your life, proceed with caution and ask yourself, "Will my decision help or hinder my life, sense of fulfillment, and well-being in the long run?"

Preparation, Presentation, Participation

One of the greatest responsibilities of a parent is to prepare and encourage her children to be wise. In Proverbs, Solomon tells how his father, David, encouraged him to seek after wisdom while he was still young ("tender"). (See First Kings 2:1-9 and First Chronicles 28–29 for David's full charge to his son.) This encouragement prompted Solomon to ask God for wisdom above everything else (see 1 Kings 3:9). Wisdom can be passed on from parents to children, from generation to generation. The wisdom that is passed on is the best preparation for full participation in a fulfilling life, because ultimately, all wisdom comes from God. True, parents can only "urge" their children to turn to Him. Even if your parents never taught you in this way, God's Word can function as a loving and compassionate mother or father to you. You can learn from the Scriptures and then create a legacy of wisdom to pass on to your own children.

Benjamin Franklin once said, "It is not so important how you begin your life, it's how you end your life." No one is born with wisdom. If you want wisdom, you must go after it. It takes resolve—a determination not to abandon the search once you begin, no matter how difficult the road may become. This is not a once-in-a-lifetime step; it is a daily process of choosing between two paths, that of the wicked or that of the righteous.

Get wisdom, get understanding: forget it not; neither decline from the words of my mouth. Forsake her not, and she shall preserve thee: love her and she shall keep thee. Wisdom is the principal thing; therefore get wisdom: and with all thy getting get understanding (Proverbs 4:5-7).

Those who do not study their own history are doomed to repeat it. When we do not reflect back on our own lives, as well as upon the lives of our foreparents, with a spirit of examination, scrutiny, and contemplation, we are doomed to repeat a pattern of poor choices and mistakes. David, after many mistakes and poor choices, reflected back on his own life. As a result of what he "saw," he was prompted to pass on to his young son Solomon that seeking God's wisdom was the most important choice he could make in his life. Solomon learned the lesson well. When God appeared to the new king (Solomon) and offered to fulfill any request, Solomon chose wisdom above all else (see 1 Kings 3:9). We should also make God's wisdom our first choice.

God's wisdom includes insight and understanding. We can boldly ask for wisdom today through prayer (see Jas. 1:5). Wisdom means practical discernment. It begins with respect for God, leads to right living, and results in increased ability to tell right from wrong. True wisdom is not only knowledge, but also the ability to make wise decisions in difficult circumstances. Christians don't have to grope about in the dark, hoping to stumble upon answers. We can ask for God's wisdom to guide our choices. To learn Gods will, we must study His Word and ask Him to show us how to obey it. Then we must do what He tells us. Pray this prayer if you seek God's wisdom.

Lord, grant me wisdom above all things. Help me to make this a daily process. My desire is to study Your Word and obey it. Bless me that I may learn from my mistakes and choices and from the mistakes of others so that I will not be doomed to repeat them. Amen.

Coing Home Again

Some people say, "You can never go home again." But you can—in stories. You can make a "first time visit" or "revisit" a situation or circumstance through the telling and retelling of your story. We can take our stories out of the mothballs of our memory, air them out by sharing them with others, and like a dress that has been tucked away in storage and taken out, we can pass it on to someone else to be used and appreciated.

An old Hausa proverb says, "May God preserve us from 'if I had known'." When we share with others what we have learned about life—even when they seem not to listen—we help them because sometimes what is shared is not appreciated until a person "hears" it again in her memory. It is always good to listen. If we listen carefully and often, we will find that everything we encounter is something we have heard about when someone shared her experience with us. If you are silent long enough, examples and people will just arise to your mind.

Now that I am on the comfortable side of 40, I can look back on the bitter experiences of my life and say with assurance that they were the "sweetest" times that I spent with the Lord. I only know that because there is now a great distance of time from the pain of those experiences. In every adversity of my life, I have learned to look for the benefit that can come out of it. Even bad experiences offer benefits, but you have to look for them. You must "work out" learning to look for the life lesson. You must make a conscious effort to retrieve, salvage, reconstruct, reexamine, and then learn something positive and beneficial from bad choices. Mary McLeod Bethune once said:

"I haunted the city dumps and the trash piles behind hotels, retrieving discarded linen and kitchenware...broken chairs...Everything was scoured and mended. This was part of the training to salvage, to reconstruct, to make bricks with straw."

What we say and what is said to us, especially when we are children, stays with us for a longer period of time than we think, and it has a way of shaping our decisions and behavior later in life. One statement from a significant person in a child's life, can shape that child's thinking. I remember being teased in grade school about being thin. The word *skinny* pierced my soul like a hot dagger every time I heard it. That word made me shy away from crowds, and I would not raise my hand in class when I knew the right answer because I didn't want to bring undo attention to myself. Even when I grew older, the situation did not seem to improve. When I was 14, my perception of myself totally changed, based upon a statement from my mother. She said to me, "You are beautiful, Millicent." I was getting taller and taller and skinnier and skinnier, but my mother told me that I was beautiful—and I believed her.

What you "pass on" is valuable and helpful. It is time to share the secrets we need for a better, healthier life. We have been silent too long. Each year I organize a mentoring program at my church. We pair older, wiser women with younger women or girls in the church. The older women act as mentors or spiritual mothers to their "spiritual daughters" for the period of about one year. The pairs pray, talk, and interact with each other. Every person needs someone older and wiser to act as a mentor in his or her life. My greatest joy was to discover that the older women desperately wanted someone to mentor and pass on their wisdom. Older women sometimes do not look like they are valuable because they look like they are getting ready to "leave." But their richness has been stored up, and there comes a time when it must be released. We must make sure that the graveyard is not filled with the richness of what we need. We can whisper in the ear of the generation to come by passing on our stories.

Learn The Lesson, Then Receive The Blessin'

I have written other books about learning lessons from difficulties and tests in life. Some have read my books and said, "Wow, how did you endure such trials?" I hesitate before I respond to that question because I have to think hard to remember what they are talking about. When I compare the storms of my life with those of others, I do not have a feeling of amazement that I have endured such tests. If I were given the opportunity to choose my trials, I would still choose the ones Ive had; for in spite of every difficulty, I have landed on my feet. And through these trials I have learned to see below the surface of everything bad to see the good. I am able to agree with the apostle James:

My brethren, count it all joy when ye fall into divers temptations (James 1:2).

James does not say, "if" we face trials or temptations, but "when" we face them. Whenever you face trials of any kind, consider it nothing but joy because you know that the testing of your faith produces endurance; and endurance, patience; and patience, faith (see Jas. 1:3-4). James assumes that we will have trials and that it is possible to learn and be blessed and profit from them. We are not required to pretend to be happy when we face pain, but we should have a positive outlook because of the results the trials will bring. James tells us to turn our hardships into times of learning. Rough times can teach us patience.

Everyone falls. We all have crises over which we have no control. If you don't die, you will get up again. The key is, while getting up, being sensitive to learn before moving forward again. If you don't, you will experience the same fall again in another place in life. Pain is an experience that should never be wasted. If we look for the "blessin' in the lesson," we will see that pain is used by God to help us understand that we are really sharing with Christ and need to grow. Life itself teaches us. The woman who views the world at 50 the same as she did at 20 has wasted 30 years of her life. If you are experiencing trials and cannot see how anything positive can come out of it, pray this prayer.

Lord, show me today what You would have me to learn through this experience. Open up my heart and understanding to see the purpose in allowing this situation to happen. Then help me to yield to Your way of teaching so that the character of Christ can be formed in me. Amen.

Been There, Done That, Moved On

I am happy with the choices that I have made because I have tried to use every gift and ability God has given me to discern what characteristic He was trying to build in me. Dark days come to all of us. Yet discouraging days bring with them golden opportunities to learn to be kind to ourselves. Believe it or not, today offers you a hidden gift, if you are willing to search for it with thanks. The goal is to try to make some sense out of the unexplainable situations of life that cause us to question God, learn a good lesson, then move on. Yesterday is a *canceled check,* but today is a ***promissory note*** from God that morning by morning we will see new mercies.

The Lord is good to all: and His tender mercies are over all His works (Psalm 145:9).

We have all had our share and degrees of trials and tribulations. We truly admire those who endure life's beatings and triumph as better people because many of us do not always win. Some of us become bitter, some become angry, and others become totally overwhelmed. When this happens, we cannot move forward with our lives. Each of us must build the spiritual base necessary for developing a healthy mind and spirit. When the course of your life is navigated by your spirituality, you will receive help from God on your journey.

George Washington Carver once said, "There is a use for almost everything." God never plows into the soul of a person without a plan or purpose. In the life of a believer, nothing is accidental. This week begin an experiment in enlightenment. For seven days assume that nothing that happens in your daily routine is accidental. Cast a wider net. Pay close attention to your dreams and thoughts. Honor your hunches. Use discernment as the spiritual tool that it is. Be receptive and alert. See how many coincidences you accumulate in the course of a day. The more you are open to synchronicity's role in your life, the more magnetic you become to God's assistance.

You can become the architect of your own future and the curator of your own contentment when you develop the habit of not allowing yourself to become "stuck" in a place of pain and bitterness. You must move on by realizing that struggles are gifts from God that are meant to alter us. When you want to move on, here's how to make it happen.

1. Ask yourself, "What is my goal?" It may be to end a dead-end relationship, achieve a healthy body, or grow in your career. Write it down.

2. Identify action steps to help you achieve your goal. (Tell him to "get lost" today. Exercise three times a week. Take a course to enhance your job skills.) Plan each step in your weekly schedule. Write down when each action must be completed.

3. Reach out for help. Develop a support group of friends, family, and colleagues who can pray with you and provide information, advice, and contacts.

4. Encourage yourself daily. Say, "I deserve to have a happy and successful life." Then say a prayer of thanks to God for the spiritual help you are receiving to accomplish your goal.

They That Wait

One of our greatest barriers to growth is our lack of patience and inability to wait on God. God chose Joshua to lead the Israelites in the conquest of Canaan (see Josh. 11). The conquest of much of the land of Canaan seems to have happened quickly. We can read about it in one sitting, but it actually took seven years. We often expect quick changes in our lives and quick victories over sin. But our journey with God is a lifelong process, and the changes and victories may take time. It is easy to grow impatient with God and feel like giving up hope because things are moving too slowly.

I remember making my first cake. It was a disaster. I purchased the ingredients and followed the instructions for mixing and preparation for cooking. I set the oven at the appropriate temperature, put the cake in, and then began to watch the clock. I tip-toed into the kitchen every ten minutes and opened the oven door to peek at it. Mother told me not to jump up and down in the kitchen. She warned me about peeping in the oven. "Just wait patiently," she would say. "Your cake will be done at the right time." But my lack of patience made it impossible for me to obey her. I would gently open the oven door, press the top of the cake with my hand to see if it would bounce back, then close the oven door with a thud. It was not cooking fast enough for me. When the cooking time was over, Mother pulled my "first cake" from the oven. It was flat like a pancake. I followed the instructions, but I did not do so with patience. The final product was ruined because of my lack of patience and my inability to wait.

When we are close to a situation, it is difficult to see progress. But when we look back we can see that God never stopped working.

It is natural for children to trust their parents, even though parents sometimes fail to keep their promises. Our heavenly Father never makes promises that He cannot keep.

But if we hope for that we see not, then do we with patience wait for it (Romans 8:25).

Nevertheless, God's plan may take more time than we expect. Rather than acting like frustrated, impatient children as we wait for God's will to unfold, we should place our confidence in His goodness and wisdom, and then wait patiently.

In frustration, Job jumped to the false conclusion that God was out to get him. Wrong assumptions lead to wrong conclusions. We dare not take our limited experiences and jump to conclusions about life in general. If you find yourself doubting God, remember that you do not have all the facts. God wants only the best for your life.

Truly God is good to Israel, even to such as are of a clean heart (Psalm 73:1).

Many people endure great pain, but ultimately they find some greater good came from it. When you are struggling, do not assume the worst. God sees the total picture of your life. Struggle is God's invitation to grow. It gives us a deeper understanding and level of appreciation of God's mercy and peace. Struggle gets your attention. Otherwise, you would miss the lesson. There is the old adage, "If I knew then what I know now." But "then" would have been too soon for you to know it! Think about this example. Let's say that you always wanted a new car. You work overtime and save your money faithfully. When you finally get the car, you enjoy it, polishing and washing it every day. On the other hand, if someone just gives you a car, the appreciation level is not there because there is no emotional investment. The bottom line is, how would you recognize and appreciate God's peace unless you underwent struggle?

Even the strongest people get tired at times, but God's power and strength never diminish. He is never too tired or too busy to help and listen. God's strength is our source of strength. When you feel all of life crashing down upon you and cannot go another step, remember that you can call upon God to renew your strength.

But they that wait upon the Lord shall renew their strength; they shall mount up with wings as eagles; they shall run and not be weary; and they shall walk, and not faint (Isaiah 40:31).

We all need regular times to listen to God. In my own life, the times that I was compelled to listen most were during those times when I was waiting for God to answer or move in a certain way. Waiting for the Lord is expecting that His promise of strength will help us to rise above life's distractions and difficulties. Listening to God helps us to be prepared for when He speaks to us, to be patient when He asks us to wait, and to expect Him to fulfill promises we find in His Word. If you are in a posture of waiting and expectation, pray this prayer:

> *Lord, strengthen me in my time of impatience and frustration. Help me to know that You have a plan for my life and that You are working everything out for my good. Give me the grace I need to wait. Open my spiritual ears to hear Your voice and to follow Your leading. Amen.*

So That Was the Point

Before we die, we will each come to the point where we will look up and say "so that was the point," as long as we allow God to teach us the lessons we need to learn through the guidance of the Holy Spirit. The Holy Spirit will guide us to the knowledge that it was all about God's ultimate goal for us—to make us like Christ.

> *Beloved, now are we the sons of God, and it doth not yet appear what we shall be: but we know that, when He shall appear, we shall be like Him; for we shall see Him as He is* (1 John 3:2).

There is value in settling down and looking back over one's life. The combination, measure, and mixture of what happens in life and what you learn from it is what shapes you into the person that you are. Middle age should be a time of life that everyone looks forward to. Life is an "acquired taste."

Life can be likened unto a banquet table set before hungry persons. The table is filled with such culinary delights as the sweet taste of success and achievement as well as the bitter herbs of pain, failure, and disappointment. Just like the person sitting at a banquet table spread with every type of food, we too are presented with a plethora, or superabundance, of choices in life. One must select the proper utensil—spoon, knife, or fork—in order to properly sample each food. The soup must be scooped up with a soup spoon, and the spaghetti must be rolled on a fork. The meat must be cut with a sharp knife, while the bread must be eaten from the hand. The way in which we approach life and the choices we make will determine our level of success and enjoyment of life. Life is an acquired taste. Every experience must be savored slowly and carefully so that the essence of every lesson to be learned draws us closer to God.

As we analyze every experience that we have had in life, we come to the conclusion that Solomon, "the preacher," was right:

Let us hear the conclusion of the whole matter: Fear God, and keep His commandments: for this is the whole duty of man (Ecclesiastes 12:13).

His conclusion was that everything apart from God is empty, hollow, and meaningless. Solomon looked back on his life, much of which was lived apart from God. Ecclesiastes, Solomon's written sermon, is his analysis of life's experiences and a critical essay about its meaning. In Ecclesiastes, Solomon shows us that we should enjoy life with all its sweet and bitter moments. But this does not exempt us from obeying God's commands. We should search for purpose and meaning in life. But purpose and meaning cannot be found in human endeavors. We should acknowledge the evil, foolishness, and injustice in life, yet maintain a positive attitude and strong faith in God. No matter what mysteries and apparent contradictions life may hold, every one of us must work toward the single purpose of knowing God. Knowing God takes time, commitment, and effort.

An Exercise in Futility

Plato said, "An unexamined life is not worth living." In Ecclesiastes, Solomon takes us on a mental journey through his life, and he explains how everything he tried, tested, or tasted was useless (see Eccles. 2:11), irrational (see Eccles. 2:17), pointless (see Eccles. 4:8), foolish (see Eccles. 4:16), and empty (see Eccles. 6:12)—an exercise in futility. And, remember, these words came from one who "had it all"—tremendous power, wisdom, and wealth. After this biographical tour, Solomon makes his triumphant conclusion that the entire duty of man is to "fear God and keep His commandments." For God will judge us for everything we do, including every hidden thing, good or bad (see Eccles. 12:13-14).

When Solomon became king, he asked God for wisdom, and he became the wisest man in the world.

Give me now wisdom and knowledge, that I may go out and come in before this people: for who can judge this Thy people, that is so great? And God said to Solomon, because this was in thine heart, and thou hast not asked riches, wealth, or honour, nor the life of thine enemies, neither yet hast asked long life: but has asked wisdom and knowledge for thyself... (2 Chronicles 1:10-11).

Solomon studied, taught, judged, and wrote. Kings and leaders from other nations came to Jerusalem to learn from him. But with all his practical insight on life, Solomon failed to heed his own advice. At the end of his life, he looked back with an attitude of humility and repentance. He examined the world as he had experienced it, hoping to spare his readers the bitterness of learning through personal experience that everything apart from God is empty, hollow, and meaningless.

Trivial Pursuit

Solomon had a purpose in writing skeptically and pessimistically. Near the end of his life, he looked back at what was "left over," and most of it seemed futile and trivial. A common belief was that only good people prospered and that only the wicked suffered, but that had not proven true in his experiences. Solomon tried everything and achieved much, only to find that nothing apart from God made him happy.

Solomon conducted his search for life's meaning as an experiment. He first tried pursuing pleasure. He started grand public works programs, bought slaves, had many wives and concubines, set his mind on complex matters, became extremely wealthy, organized musical groups, and supported the arts. But none of these things gave him the satisfaction that he was seeking. Some of the pleasures Solomon sought were wrong, and some were worthy, but even the worthy pursuits were futile when he pursued them as an end in themselves. We must look beyond our activities to the reason we do them. Is your goal in life to search for meaning or to search for God who gives meaning?

An Elusive Goal

Life's experiences are not always happy. But the world tells us to demand happiness, do all we can to attain it, and make personal satisfaction our chief goal. Solomon, writing about his own life, discovered that his wealth, power, position, wives, and accomplishments did not make him happy. Happiness is an elusive goal because people and circumstances change quickly.

I remember my first vacation in the Bahamas. I was only 21 years old. I had never flown on an airplane and had never traveled farther than a few states in the South to see relatives during summer vacation. On the afternoon that we arrived in the Bahamas, I was so happy and so excited. I enjoyed the warmth and excitement of a tropical island. I wanted to freeze those moments in time. I thought that was true happiness. Then the sky began to cloud over, and that perfect, sunny afternoon became filled with a gentle, tropical rain. Then night fell. My friends began to retire to their hotel rooms for rest. An overwhelming feeling of loneliness came over me, and suddenly, I wanted to go home more than anything else in the world. There was no television in my room, and I had finished reading the two books I brought with me. The boredom was almost unbearable. I could not get to sleep, and the sound of the ocean made the silence of the night even more haunting. That night I vowed never to return to the islands again.

People and circumstances change quickly; nothing ever remains the same. Depending on outward situations and circumstances to bring us lasting happiness is a mistake because life is so changeable. True and lasting happiness comes from pleasing God. Thus, happiness cannot be achieved; it can only be received through a right relationship with God, because only God really knows what is best for us. If you are chasing after happiness, you will never find it. If you are seeking God, you will find endless joy.

Spiritual Toothpicks

A gracious hostess makes sure that there are toothpicks on the table or at strategic places for her guests to find after a sumptuous meal. Men and women alike can be seen digging and probing between their teeth trying to dislodge the last morsels of food lodged there. They try to be polite and use good manners. But there is just no way to pick your teeth politely in public. I do not remember really needing a toothpick after meals when I was younger. But something must happen to the teeth and gums as one ages, because I now find myself carrying dental floss in my handbag. Perhaps I am more keenly aware now of the importance of dental hygiene and oral health. I was raised to always conduct myself as a lady in public, so I always excuse myself to a ladies room when I have to floss.

It is a good thing to go back over your life every now and then to think about "your stories." Enjoy the spiritual meal all over again. Look at the "leftovers" on the table. And when you sit back satisfied, remember, if you probe long enough you can always find a few remaining morsels of wisdom lodged between the information of those stories that you can chew on again. The morsel is not the meal itself; it is only a "tidbit" or "scrap" of what it was, but it is tasty just the same.

Enjoy the "spiritual toothpicks" that follow, and allow them to guide you through a month of spiritual growth. These sweet morsels of wisdom will encourage you to reexamine your experiences against the backdrop of what you have read. Pick at those tight places. There is always something else to dig for. You may choose to swallow the morsel or discard it, but acknowledge that it is there. The sweet morsels of wisdom and godly advice from the lessons of life will help you "get it together" and "keep it together."

Day 1   Drop a habit that has kept you from reaching your potential.

Day 2   Pick a motivating word for the day, e.g., *love, hope, support, forgiveness.*

Day 3   Pray.

Day 4   Hang up a happy photo of yourself.

Day 5   Read about someone who failed many times before succeeding, such as Thomas Edison.

Day 6   Seek the sacred in the ordinary.

Day 7   Count your blessings today. What would it take to convince you that you already have everything that you need to be happy?

Day 8   Acknowledge the angels; believe in miracles.

Day 9   Live with obstacles.

Day 10 Kiss the ground.

Day 11 Listen to your life.

Day 12 Try not to panic.

Day 13 Pay attention.

Day 14 Smile in a mirror for one minute.

Day 15 Hug someone.

Day 16 Get ruthlessly honest with yourself.

Day 17 Say out loud, "The world is blessed to have me."

Day 18 Take time out.

Day 19 Cash in on "favors" owed.

Day 20 Learn something new.

Day 21 Squash the "good-old-days" bug.

Day 22 Designate a formal weekly or monthly self-assessment day.

Day 23 Rehearse the steps to success in your mind before you begin.

Day 24 Expect yourself to succeed.

Day 25 Get more fresh air. Go on a weekend retreat, the type that energizes you the most.

Day 26 Check for internal conflicts and self-sabotage.

Day 27 Find a mentor.

Day 28 Make sure that at least one of your best friends is highly motivated in the same way you are.

Day 29 Know your boundaries.

Day 30 Get away from problem thinking and embrace outcome thinking.

Day 31 Follow these two rules: a) Get started; b) Keep going.

Knowledge Is a Tool

Solomon highlights two kinds of wisdom in the book of Ecclesiastes: *human knowledge* (which includes reasoning or philosophy) and the *wisdom that comes from God*. When human knowledge ignores God, it only highlights our problems because it cannot provide answers that need an eternal perspective and solution.

After writing that everything is futile (see Eccles. 1:2-11), Solomon recorded that even his great wisdom could not offer the satisfaction that he was seeking. Wisdom, in itself, brought grief rather than satisfaction. Knowledge is simply a tool for living life better, not the end for which we were created. The more you understand, the more pain and difficulty you will experience. For example, the more you know, the more imperfection you see around you, and the more you observe, the more evil becomes evident. I remember being quite fearless as a younger woman. I knew that evil existed in the world, but I somehow thought that horrendous crimes and tragedies were calamities that happened to other people. Murder and assault and muggings were terrible things that happened to people on the evening news. One summer, I had a job at a hospital. I had to take several modes of public transportation at all hours of the night to get to work. I would often walk alone in the dark, dangerous, underground subway corridors of north Philadelphia at one or two o'clock in the morning. I thought nothing of it. I walked along, almost skipping, as young women do, with a handbag full of money swinging on my arm. I was completely unaware of what and who was around me. I am keenly aware of God's continued hedge of protection that was around me during those times. I was never mugged, robbed, or assaulted in what was one of Philadelphia's most dangerous urban areas. Now that I am older, wiser, and have a greater understanding and knowledge of the evil and imperfection of the world around me, I seldom travel alone, never take public transportation at night, never travel without a car phone, and never allow my children to leave home unsupervised or unchaperoned. I am acutely aware of everything that goes on around me. As you set out with Solomon to find the meaning of life, you must be ready to feel more, think more, question more, hurt more, and do more.

Healed on The Way

Faith is a journey. There are blessings and sacrifices made along the way. As we travel that long, tedious distance, there are wounds that we all encounter along the way. There is a time in each of our lives when we realize that the purpose of the journey was to experience the wounds, confront them, learn from them, and then get healed on the way. Wounds—everyone has them:

- Wounds of the home—separation, divorce, abuse, lack of intimacy, financial struggles.
- Wounds of the head—psychological wounds caused by racism, sexism, classism, lack of opportunity.
- Wounds of the heart—brokenness, abandonment, disappointment, mistrust, lack of commitment.

Trauma is a common denominator of every human life. How you work to find ways to balance the equation of experiencing trauma and learning from it is your life choice.

I remember struggling through a statistics course in college. I was an excellent student and always found education to be interesting, challenging, and fairly easy. But math always threw me for a loop because it was so abstract and theoretical. Other students were sailing through the tests and getting A's and B's, while I was laying hands on myself and anointing my pencil with oil before every test in the hope of getting a C. Then I came to grips with the fact that if others could succeed in math, so could I. I knew I had to put forth effort and make personal sacrifices. I took statistics because I was forced to; it was a requirement of the curriculum. So I applied myself. I missed many outings with friends and other social activities. I spent hours trying and failing and trying again. My late evening hours were spent with my head buried in a math book, but when my final exam came along I "aced the test." What a journey. A failing grade in statistics could have resulted in a low rank in my graduating class, which could have had a profound affect on my career and desire to go on to higher education.

Certain wounding situations we experience in life are not of our choosing. There are certain situations and circumstances in life that are custom designed by God. As I struggled through my statistics course, I learned how to take over-whelming difficulty, confront my problem head-on, design a strategy, work hard, and finally enjoy the success of reaching my goal. I couldn't wait to offer myself as a tutor to help other students coming along who would struggle as I did. I was excited about being able to "pass on" what I had learned.

Barriers to Believing

God has a plan for all people. Thus, He provides cycles of life and work for us to do. But we face many problems that seem to contradict God's plan. These should not be barriers to believing in Him, but rather they are opportunities to discover that without God life's problems offer no lasting solutions. Timing is important. Solomon says that all the experiences of life are appropriate at certain times.

To every thing there is a season, and a time to every purpose under the heaven (Ecclesiastes 3:1).

The secret to peace with God is to discover, accept, and appreciate God's perfect timing. The ability to appreciate and learn from a mistake depends, to a large extent, upon your attitude. Work becomes toil when you lose the sense of purpose God intended for it. Every difficult situation we encounter in our lives has a God-given purpose. When we understand that God has a purpose for everything that He allows to happen in our lives, we can enjoy the journey of faith even as we struggle and hurt along the way. We can enjoy the journey if we do the following:

- Remember that God has a plan and has already equipped us for certain tasks.
- Realize that yielding to God's plan is a personal decision that only you can make.

God's eternal plan is that we should fear Him. *Fear* does not mean to cringe in terror, but to respect, revere, rely on, and stand in awe of Him because of who He is. Purpose in life begins with *whom* we know, not what we know or how good we are. It is impossible to fulfill your God-given purpose unless you fear God and give Him first place in your life.

Eternal Values

Solomon is not a dreary pessimist. He encourages us to enjoy life and rejoice in every day but to remember that eternity is far longer than a person's life span (see Eccles. 11:7–12:14). The wise person does not just think about the moment and its impact. She takes the long-range view from eternity. Approach any decision you make in life from an eternal perspective—consider its impact ten years from now and into eternity. Live with the attitude that, although life is short, we can live with God forever. It is easy to forget how short life really is. Realizing that life is short helps us to use the little time that we have more wisely. It helps us concentrate on using our lives for eternal good, not just for the pleasure of the moment.

So teach us to number our days, that we may apply our hearts unto wisdom (Psalm 90:12).

When I was in elementary school, I often heard adults talk about how life was so short. That statement always annoyed me because I could not understand what they were talking about. To me, the days seemed to be dragging. Monday was the longest day of the week, and getting to the weekend was a painful journey. At the age of 12, I felt like I had been alive forever. Now that I am on the comfortable side of 40, I can look back and agree with James:

Whereas ye know not what shall be on the morrow. For what is your life? It is even a vapour, that appeareth for a little time, and then vanisheth away (James 4:14).

Time seems to speed up the older we get. I have the same zest for life and energy I had at 21, but when I gaze at myself in the early morning light, I get a glimpse of my mother and realize that I am getting older. Life is short, no matter how long we live. Don't be deceived into thinking that you have lots of remaining time to live for Christ, to enjoy your loved ones, or to do what you know you should do. Live for God today! Then, no matter when your life ends, you will have fulfilled God's plan for you.

How can you draw close to God? James give five suggestions:

1. Give yourself humbly to God (Jas. 4:7).
2. Realize that you need God's forgiveness and be willing to follow Him (Jas. 4:7).
3. Resist the devil. Don't allow him to entice and tempt you. Lead a pure life and let your heart be filled with God (Jas. 4:8).
4. Let there be tears of sorrow and sincere grief for your sins (Jas. 4:9).
5. Realize your worthlessness. Humble yourself before God, and He will lift you up (Jas. 4:10).

Take time to number your days by asking, "What do I want to see happen in my life before I die? What small step could I take toward that purpose today?" So go ahead—plan! It is good to have goals, but goals can disappoint us if we leave God out of them. There is no point in making plans as though God does not exist, because the future is in His hands. What would you like to be doing ten years from now? One year from now? Tomorrow? How will you react if God steps in and rearranges your plans? Plan ahead, but hang on to your plans lightly. If you put God's desires at the center of your plans, you will not be disappointed.

This life is not all there is, yet even in this life we should not pass judgment on God because we do not know the reason and purpose for everything that happens. God's plan is for us to live forever with Him. So live with eternal values in view, realizing that all your questions will one day be answered by the Creator Himself.

The Great Equalizer

Grandma was right! All people will have to stand before God and be judged for what they have done in this life. The certainty of death makes all merely human achievements futile. God has a plan for human destiny that goes beyond life and death. The reality of aging and dying reminds us of the end to come when God will judge each person's life. Because life is short, we need wisdom that is greater than this world can offer. We need the words of God. If we listen to the words of God, His wisdom spares us the bitterness of futile human experience. Human wisdom does not contain all the answers. Knowledge and education have their limits. To understand life, we need the wisdom that can only be found in God's Word—the Bible.

When I conducted my first funeral as a young pastor, God prepared me. The deceased was a cancer victim, the mother of one of my deacons. When I met her, I heard the voice of God as I shook her frail hand and said, "Hello." God whispered to me, "You will bury her in a week's time." I was shaken because my experience as a pastor at this point had involved only blessing babies and performing weddings—all the fun stuff. I had attended funerals before, but I had never been the only one in charge in ministering to a bereaved family from the shock of death to the resolve that their loved one had departed this life forever. I prayed for strength to get through the ordeal. I did not want to cry or choke on my words through the sermon or weep at the grave site, so I prayed to God for strength.

On the day of the funeral, I was a tower of strength and everything that the grieving family needed their pastor to be. As I stood there looking at the lifeless remains in the casket, I thought about the fragility and the brevity of life. I thought about the utter helplessness that we all have when death comes calling. No amount of human power can turn death away when it comes calling. Every funeral I conduct or attend now reminds me of the importance of making the best of every moment God so graciously grants us.

Solomon reminds us how easily death comes to us, how swiftly and unexpectedly we can return to the dust from which we came. Therefore, we should not act as if nothing could harm us. The silver cord, golden bowl, pitcher, and wheel symbolize how fragile life is.

> *Or ever the silver cord be loosed, or the golden bowl be broken, or the pitcher be broken at the fountain, or the wheel broken at the cistern. Then shall the dust return to the earth as it was; and the spirit shall return unto God who gave it* (Ecclesiastes 12:6-7).

All souls and spirits are in the keeping of God. Stripped of the spirit God has given us, our bodies return to dust. Stripped of God's purpose, our work is in vain. Stripped of God's love, our service is futile. We must put God first *over* all that we do and *in* all that we do, for without Him we have nothing. Knowing that life is futile without God motivates the wise person to find God. All people will have to stand before God and be judged for what they did in this life. We will not be able to use life's inconsistencies as an excuse for failing to live properly. To live properly, we need to observe the following items:

- Recognize that human effort apart from God is futile.
- Put God first—now.
- Receive every good thing as a gift from God.
- Realize that God will judge both evil and good.
- Know that God will judge the quality of every person's life. We must view life as a preparation for eternity, knowing that every work of humankind will be brought into judgment, including every secret thing—whether it be good or evil.

You Are What You Eat

Any health enthusiast knows the importance of a healthy diet. A healthy diet produces a healthy body. In order to maintain a healthy lifestyle, one must, ideally, eat properly throughout his or her lifetime. It is not enough to eat fresh fruits and vegetables, lean meat, fish, poultry, whole grain products, milk, and juices during the growing years only to abandon yourself later in life to a diet of fast foods, snacks, sodas, and sugary desserts. The benefits of healthy eating habits during one's younger years can be almost completely destroyed by poor eating habits in later years. Even though each season of life brings with it a new set of health issues and challenges, there is still no substitute for a consistently healthy way of eating. After all, you are what you eat.

Every season of life brings with it a new set of problems and challenges. A diet of consistent study of God's Word keeps you spiritually healthy and strong and gives you a storehouse of positive ways to address issues and handle crises that arise in your life. Most of us spent years in Sunday school as young children and teens. We learned memory verses and Bible stories that remain a permanent part of our memory today. Now that we are no longer children, we need a greater understanding and deeper revelation of God's Word. That is why it is important to remain a student of the Word throughout your lifetime. An adult cannot be properly spiritually nourished from teaching of the Word of God that is meant for a child or a new believer. When my two children were newborns, I was amazed at how quickly they grew and how healthy they were from a diet of only milk. But as they continued to grow, their nutritional needs changed. Milk was and still is a necessary part of their diet, but milk alone is not enough. In order to continue to grow healthily, they need meat, vegetables, breads, and other healthy foods. Likewise, if we are to become stable, mature believers who need proper nourishment from the Word of God, we cannot subsist on "kids' meals." We need adult entrées from God's Word. Peter speaks of his readers being born again (see 1 Pet. 1:23). Then he tells them how to grow as newborn babes in Christ.

As newborn babes, desire the sincere milk of the word, that ye may grow thereby (1 Peter 2:2).

We grow by taking the unadulterated milk of the Word of God, the pure doctrines of the Bible, as recorded in the New Testament, and applying it to our life. One characteristic all children share is that they want to grow up to be like the "big kids" or like their parents. When we are born again, we become spiritual infants. If we are healthy, we will yearn to grow. How sad it is that some people never grow up. The need for milk is a natural instinct for a baby as well as a sign of growth. We all need the basics in order to grow. Once we see our need for God's Word and begin to find nourishment in Christ, our spiritual appetite will increase, and we will start to mature. When we begin to mature in Christ, the "milk" of the Word is no longer enough for us. We need the "meat" of God's Word, which is a more complete understanding of faith and how to live more effectively for Christ.

For every one that useth milk is unskillful in the Word of righteousness: for he is a babe. But strong meat belongeth to them that are of full age... (Hebrews 5:13-14).

I enjoy eating out with my family, so I always set aside at least one day a week to enjoy a meal at a restaurant with my children. The ordering of our food is always preceded by a lengthy discussion about "who can have what." To prevent my children from "over ordering" and ending up with a lot of leftovers, I always limit them to the selections from the kids' menu. The kids' menu contains "kids' meals," foods that are specifically tailored to the nutritional needs and tastes of a youngster. "The adult entrées," I tell them, "are for adult tastes and appetites." We cannot rely on what we learned about God when we were young children once we become adults. What we learned when we were youngsters was good. What we learned in Sunday school was tailored to the spiritual needs of a youngster. Now that we are adults, we have adult problems and adult challenges. We must be well-equipped to do spiritual warfare. Paul said that when he was a child, he spoke, thought, and reasoned like a child, but when he became an adult he had to put an end to childish things (see 1 Cor. 13:11).

In order to meet the challenges of adulthood and grow spiritually healthy as an adult, there is no substitute for consistent, systematic study of God's Word. It is not enough to have personal, private, individual Bible study on your own because the possibility of error is so great. Instead one must commit himself or herself to a church where the Word of God is being preached and taught by an anointed and learned teacher.

You must have a mature knowledge of Scripture. When you are confronted with a difficult life situation a few random Scriptures, that you remember from your childhood and that are not directly related to your problem, are not enough. You must be knowledgeable enough about the Word of God so you can put the "right word" with the "right situation." For example, if you are confronted with a situation that could result in financial ruin, it is not enough to know "Jesus wept" and "the Lord is my Shepherd," even though these are good verses to know (see Jn. 11:35; Ps. 23:1). You must know Scriptures that specifically address your situation. You must have a thorough knowledge and understanding of the Word of God so that you can encourage yourself and get God's direction by putting the right word with the right situation such as:

> *Bring ye all the tithes into the storehouse, that there may be meat in Mine house, and prove Me now herewith, saith the Lord of hosts, if I will not open you the windows of heaven, and pour you out a blessing that there shall not be room enough to receive it* (Malachi 3:10).

> *...he which soweth sparingly shall reap also sparingly; and he which soweth bountifully shall reap also bountifully...God loveth a cheerful giver* (2 Corinthians 9:6-7).

> *Give, and it shall be given unto you; good measure, pressed down, and shaken together and running over, shall men give into your bosom. For with the same measure that ye mete withal it shall be measured to you again* (Luke 6:38).

Speed Bumps

Problems are speed bumps on the highway of life. Speed bumps do not bring the car to a halt. They only slow the vehicle down to a slower speed. The purpose of the speed bump is to slow the driver down in order to avoid what could be a tragic, fatal accident, which could destroy not only the life of the driver of the vehicle but other innocent persons as well. The speed bump can be annoying. But looking at it in a more positive light, it forces the driver to slow down and look around and observe his or her surroundings. The tree up ahead or the on-coming car full of unsuspecting passengers might have brought tragedy, but the speed bump caused you to "take notice."

I thank God for every speed bump in my life. Had it not been for those annoying little mounds here and there, I would have sped along down life's highway at speeds of 100 mph, destined for destruction. Problems are the speed bumps that give pace to life. When we slow down, we are given the opportunity to look around, and when we look around, we learn. Everything can speak to our soul and teach us if we are willing to pay attention and listen. Every virtuoso knows that it is the pauses in between the notes where the art resides. You must never forget to pause, especially when the distractions of daily life deplete your energy. Pause to reflect, to evaluate, to think, to contemplate what's working in your life and what's not, so that you can "talk to God" about it and make changes for the better. My grandmother would talk to God in prayer. Boy, would she talk to God—like He was her uncle. "God, now you know what I need, Lord," she would say. She deliberated on every word. Then she would pause in her prayer; God was answering her back. I learned from my grandmother how to be straightforward and simple in my prayers. I used to feel guilty because I prayed in bed. I thought out of respect that maybe I should assume a more formal prayer position like kneeling on my knees, pressing my hands together, and lowering my eyes. But I learned that the best prayers are those that are honest and sincere wherever you are. So I talk to God in the morning in bed and in the evening in bed. Start seeking order within by "book-ending" your day with simple prayer and honest reflection—first thing in the morning and last thing at night.

A Thorough Job

At the end of every good meal there is the drudgery of cleaning the dirty dishes. Washing dishes is not merely rubbing a few plates and saucers with a wet rag. My mother demanded that a complete and thorough job always be done. Washing dishes meant scrubbing the plates, glasses, cutlery, pots, and pans with the hottest water tolerable. It also meant sweeping the floor, wiping the stove with steel wool, and finally, wiping dry the water stains left in the sink. "Now that's a thorough job," Mom would say. When I was growing up I got lots of practice in the art of dishwashing. Most girls become experts by the age of 13. I have had my share of puddles on the floor and suds in my hair. I remember my mother showing me the "system," as she called it for washing dishes in an efficient and timely manner. "You've got to be organized," she would say, "get yourself a system and stick to it, that way you can get the job done and move on to better things.'' I followed my mother's good advice. I would stack the dishes, fill the sink with water, fluff up the soap bubbles, roll my sleeves up, and get to work. I always washed glasses first because they had less grease and were easiest to clean. Next came the plates and saucers, then the utensils. The pots and pans were saved for last. When the job was done, I put everything away neatly in cabinets where they remained until they were needed again.

Now that you have come to the end of this spiritual feast and savored what you have learned, do a complete, thorough job of putting what you have learned away neatly until it is needed again by keeping a journal.

Do the "Write" Thing

Personal reflection and self-initiated feedback can boost motivation, so write down your feelings, concerns, dreams, progress, and private thoughts in a journal. Review your journal often, and you will gain an appreciation for your progress and yourself. But always remember, tell the truth.

To begin a journal is to embark upon a journey. Sometimes that journey is into the past—a childhood experience, a pivotal life event, a tender moment with someone you love. Sometimes that journey is into the future—battle plans for an upcoming project, strategies for handling a potential problem or heading off a crisis. And sometimes the journal itself is a vehicle for a journey. We transport ourselves into a new self-understanding by putting things into perspective, blowing off steam, cheering ourselves up, articulating dreams, and giving ourselves encouragement within the covers of our book. In our writings, we can explore what nurtures us and what gives us pleasure or satisfaction.

But a journal does not necessarily need to be a tunnel to the past, a freeway to the future, or a bridge to greater self-understanding. A journal can also simply be a road map of the day's events, of people met or to meet, things to do and things done, hopes, desires, fears, questions. A journal can be all of the above at once or at different times. So much good happens to us, but in the rush of daily life we often fail to notice or acknowledge it. Writing it down focuses our attention on how we view the experiences of our life. In each moment that passes, we can choose love over fear, peace over conflict, confidence over doubt. Each day offers the gift of being a special occasion if we can simply learn the lesson that life wants to teach us.

Writing can be a great outlet for our stress and a way to express thoughts and feelings that we find difficult to share. I have often used journal writing as a way to get my "life in order." I admit that there are things that I write in a journal that I would never verbalize or share with anyone. My secrets are safe in my writings. Journal writing, which after all is a kind of autobiography, has a long tradition among African-Americans. Slave narratives, memoirs, and autobiographies have formed a literary landscape and bear witness to our spiritual strength and our complexity. These writings preserve stories that would have been lost as generations grew old and died. Keeping a journal makes each and every one of us a custodian of our people by bearing witness to the world around us and, more importantly, by documenting our impressions of our own lives for the future. Black men and women have never hesitated to put pen to paper to preserve their powerful stories, to plan their future, and to record the facts of their existence.

The ancient women in my family seldom wrote their stories down, but they had an extraordinarily creative way of telling them. My grandmother's stories, especially, were to my life what a comet is to a darkened sky. Her words of wisdom shone brightly; their insight and intuitiveness were as singular as a comet's trail. Just like her collard greens, her stories were well-seasoned with wit and religion. Her remarkable talent for telling stories illumined not only my life, but the life of every young woman who listened.

Do the "write" thing. Keeping a journal means keeping track, and when you share your stories you pass the baton to those who can benefit from your experiences. Pull your stories out of the mothballs of obscurity. Air them out. Pick up your pen, and bear witness to the wonderful way that God is at work in your life. Then pass it on!

Other
Destiny Image ***titles***
you will enjoy reading

CRASHING SATAN'S PARTY
by Dr. Millicent Thompson.
Don't let satan hinder the power of God from working in your life any longer! In this book you'll discover the strategies and devices the enemy uses against you. Too many of us attribute our troubles to God when they are really of the devil. The adversary is subtle and delights in deception. We must be able to recognize *who* is doing *what* in our lives so that we can react according to God's Word. Learn how to destroy the works of the enemy. You can crash satan's party and overcome!
ISBN 1-56043-268-3 $10.99p

DON'T DIE IN THE WINTER...
by Dr. Millicent Thompson.
Why do we go through hard times? Why must we suffer pain? In *Don't Die in the Winter...* Dr. Thompson explains the spiritual seasons and cycles that people experience. A spiritual winter is simply a season that tests our growth. We need to endure our winters, for in the plan of God, spring always follows winter!
ISBN 1-56043-558-5 $8.99p

HOW TO RAISE CHILDREN OF DESTINY
by Dr. Patricia Morgan.
This groundbreaking book highlights the intricate link between the rise of young prophets, priests, and kings in the Body of Christ as national leaders and deliverers, and the salvation of a generation.
ISBN 1-56043-134-2 $9.99p

THE BATTLE FOR THE SEED
by Dr. Patricia Morgan.
The dilemma facing young people today is a major concern for all parents. This important book of the 90's shows God's way to change the condition of the young and advance God's purpose for every nation into the next century.
ISBN 1-56043-099-0 $9.99p

Available at your local Christian bookstore.
Internet: http://www.reapernet.com
Prices subject to change without notice.

B6:28

Exciting titles
by Myles Munroe

UNDERSTANDING YOUR POTENTIAL

This is a motivating, provocative look at the awesome potential trapped within you, waiting to be realized. This book will cause you to be uncomfortable with your present state of accomplishment and dissatisfied with resting on your past success.
ISBN 1-56043-046-X $9.99p

RELEASING YOUR POTENTIAL

Here is a complete, integrated, principles-centered approach to releasing the awesome potential trapped within you. If you are frustrated by your dreams, ideas, and visions, this book will show you a step-by-step pathway to releasing your potential and igniting the wheels of purpose and productivity.
ISBN 1-56043-072-9 $9.99p

MAXIMIZING YOUR POTENTIAL

Are you bored with your latest success? Maybe you're frustrated at the prospect of retirement. This book will refire your passion for living! Learn to maximize the God-given potential lying dormant inside you through the practical, integrated, and penetrating concepts shared in this book. Go for the max—die empty!
ISBN 1-56043-105-9 $9.99p

IN PURSUIT OF PURPOSE

Best-selling author Myles Munroe reveals here the key to personal fulfillment: purpose. We must pursue purpose because our fulfillment in life depends upon our becoming what we were born to be and do. *In Pursuit of Purpose* will guide you on that path to finding purpose.
ISBN 1-56043-103-2 $9.99p

SINGLE, MARRIED, SEPARATED & LIFE AFTER DIVORCE

Written by best-selling author Myles Munroe, this is one of the most important books you will ever read. It answers hard questions with compassion, biblical truth, and even a touch of humor. It, too, is rapidly becoming a best-seller.
ISBN 1-56043-094-X $9.99p

B6:2

Exciting titles
by T.D. Jakes

CAN YOU STAND TO BE BLESSED?

You ask God to bless you and difficulties arise. Why? This book will release the hidden strength within you to go on in God, fulfilling the destiny He has for you. The way to this success is full of twists and turns, yet you can make it through to incredible blessing in your life. The only question left will be, *Can You Stand to Be Blessed?*
ISBN 1-56043-801-0 $9.99p

CAN YOU STAND TO BE BLESSED? WORKBOOK

Are you ready to unlock the inner strength to go on in God? This workbook will help you apply the book's principles to your life. Appropriate for individual or small group study.
ISBN 1-56043-812-6 $7.99p

NAKED AND NOT ASHAMED

With a powerful anointing, Bishop T.D. Jakes challenges us to go below the surface and become completely and honestly vulnerable before God and man. In relationships, in prayer, in ministry—we need to be willing to be open and transparent. Why do we fear? God already knows us, but He cannot heal our hidden hurts unless we expose them to Him. Only then can we be *Naked and Not Ashamed*!
ISBN 1-56043-835-5 $9.99p

NAKED AND NOT ASHAMED WORKBOOK

This is no ordinary workbook! A companion to *Naked and Not Ashamed*, this "Application Journal" has been carefully created to help you grasp and apply the principles found in the book. In it you'll be asked to do more than mark answers. You'll be called upon to grapple with difficult issues—because God is determined to make you whole, strong, and anointed in His service!
ISBN 1-56043-259-4 $7.99p

WOMAN, THOU ART LOOSED!

This book offers healing to hurting single mothers, insecure women, and battered wives; and hope to abused girls and women in crisis! Hurting women around the nation—and those who minister to them—are devouring the compassionate truths in Bishop T.D. Jakes' *Woman, Thou Art Loosed!*
ISBN 1-56043-100-8 $9.99p

WOMAN, THOU ART LOOSED! WORKBOOK

Whether studying in a group or as an individual, this workbook will help you learn and apply the truths found in *Woman, Thou Art Loosed!* If you're searching to increase your spiritual growth, then this workbook is for you.
ISBN 1-56043-810-X $7.99p

Available at your local Christian bookstore.

Internet: http://www.reapernet.com

Prices subject to change without notice.

B6:29